IMPR

IMPRESSIONS

Martin Wells Knapp

Tyndale House Publishers, Inc., Wheaton, Illinois

All Scripture quotations are taken from the King James Version.

First edition published 1892
Revivalist Press, Cincinnati, Ohio

First printing, Tyndale House edition, June 1984

Library of Congress Catalog Card Number 83-51868
ISBN 0-8423-1601-9, paper

CONTENTS

One
The Origin of Impressions   7

Two
Impressions from Below: Satan's Deceptions   19

Three
Impressions from Below: Satan's Judges   27

Four
Impressions from Below: Results of Following Them   39

Five
Impressions: How to Test Them   49

Six
Impressions from Above: Divine Guidance Guaranteed   65

Seven
Impressions from Above: How to Be Led by Them   75

Eight
Practical Applications   85

Nine
Convictions from Above: Results of Being Led by Them   97

Ten
Man's Perfect Model   109

The Origin of Impressions

An impression may be defined as "an influence on purposes, feelings, or actions."

While we are free to choose the right or wrong, yet we are continually acted upon by influences which impress in different ways. Some of them come silently as the sunshine; others come like the lightning's stroke or thunder's peal; others like gentle zephyrs, and some like the devastating tornado.

Every impression has a source. Back of all operating second causes there is with each impression a designing mind which is the source of it. God is the author of all good impressions, Satan of all that are evil.

Hence all impressions are naturally divided into two classes: (1) those from our Father, which we will call "impressions from above." These, if followed, ripen into convictions; and (2) those from the devil, which we will call "impressions from below."

IMPRESSIONS FROM ABOVE

All impressions from above originate with God. He speaks directly by His Spirit in the heart wherein He reigns. In its "secret inner chamber" He sweetly whispers the "will of God concerning us."

Under this direct impulse from within, Jesus was "led up of the Spirit into the wilderness to be tempted of the devil."

Paul was thus impelled to preach the Gospel in some places but restrained from others, and Christians in all ages have been directly impressed concerning the truth and its application to their special needs.

The Holy Spirit is the Christian's promised guide. He makes no new revelation of truth, but explains that already revealed. His guidance is always in harmony with the Bible, of which He is the author. His modes of guiding will be noticed further on. Following His leadings is one of the marks of being a true believer. "As many as are led by the Spirit of God, they are the sons of God" (Romans 8:14).

His leadings are above all others, and all others are made potent by His power. Many have written ably on His exalted offices. This work will undertake to magnify Him, by warning against voices which seek to simulate His tones by substituting impressions from below for convictions from above.

There are many different telegraph wires over which messages are transmitted from the divine mind to our own. The following are among them:

The Bible. This is God's will revealed in human language. Its impressions are divine. It speaks on every needed subject, and its general principles and specific applications of them are designed above all minor voices to so impress us that "being made wise unto salvation," whatsoever we do in word or deed shall be done solely for man's good and God's glory.

The ministry. God frequently sends special and startling messages by His ministers. Impressions made by the truth as it leaps from a glowing heart are often indelible. Many, as at Pentecost, have been "so pricked to the heart," that they have found no rest until fully surrendered to Jesus. Others have thus been comforted, or strengthened, or convicted for some special work.

Personal influence. Many messages from above are sent over this wire. The impressions thus made on my mind by letters from a dear friend awakened and led me to Jesus, and when tried in the furnace of God's afflictive fires, one of the strongest comforting impressions that came to me was caused by the following lines sent by one of earth's comforting angels:

> *In the furnace God may prove thee,*
> *Thence to bring thee forth more bright,*
> *But can never cease to love thee,*
> *Thou art precious in His sight.*
> *God is with thee,*
> *God thine everlasting light.*

Such instances like the sands of the seashore are numberless.

Prayer. One of the mightiest influences which leads Godward and heavenward is the prayer of faith. Under its power, persecuting Sauls fall blindly to the earth, the counsels of persecutors are overturned, and saints are comforted and led in ways they knew not of. Mighty is the pressure brought to bear upon the mind of the one for whom a number unite in prayer. Who is there that has not "felt" the prayers of others in their restraining or persuasive influence?

Good reading. Good books and papers are among the mightiest agencies which God is now using to impress men with His truth. Through them He is silently undermining the fortifications of the enemy, and building up His spiritual

kingdom. They have won many who were impervious to
all other appeals, and their influence is mighty and quiet,
like the laws of gravitation.

Angels. Impressions from above often come from holy
angels. The Psalmist declared that "the angel of the Lord
encampeth round about them that fear him, and delivereth
them." These, and many parallel passages in the Word
are confirmed by the express declarations in Hebrews that
they are "all ministering spirits, sent forth to minister
for them who shall be heirs of salvation."

Wise, mighty, holy, elect, and innumerable, they are
among the most powerful, yet unseen and often unappre-
ciated agencies. God has given them to "have charge"
over His people. Sometimes their special errand is to
comfort in some fiery furnace; or to cheer in some dark
lion's den; or to warn of some threatening peril; or to
deliver from prison; or to rejoice over souls newly saved;
or to announce the tidings of a Savior's birth and
resurrection; or to execute the judgments of God upon the
ungodly; or to influence a preacher's appointment, as
with Philip; or to help a seeker to obtain the gift of the
Holy Ghost, as with Cornelius; or to cheer in danger and
point to a promising future, as with Paul. In every instance
angels have human interest in their keeping, and doubtless
much more frequently than is generally thought are the
agents of impressions from above.

Dreams. "In the Bible," says the *Christian Standard*, "we
have repeated illustrations of where God led His children
'by impulses, impressions, calls, messages, or dreams,'
as well as 'by the Holy Ghost operating on all the faculties
of the mind, strengthening each to perform its function
along the lines of common sense, sound reason, and a
sanctified judgment.'

"Because we are often misled by impressions, dreams,
etc.; because Satan often uses these ways of deceiving

souls; yet it is not necessary, nor does it relieve the difficulty, to deny to the Holy Ghost the right and the fact of so leading God's people.

"Dreams may be from the devil. They may come from gluttony at the supper table. They may be generated in an overtaxed brain. They may result from many combined 'second causes.' Nevertheless, if we please, or whether we please or not, God did and can and does send dreams that we may disregard to our damage and destruction."

Few folks are so foolish as to be influenced by ordinary dreams. Yet that God has spoken to His children through special dreams no well-informed person will deny. The study of dreams is a science but little understood. Because fanatics have taken dreams born of indigestion or inspired by Satan, for divine revelation, others have gone to the opposite extreme, and like Herod with the innocents, slaughtered them by the wholesale.

For this reason few people believe in such manifestations, and according to their faith, so it is to them. The antidote for fanaticism from reliance on them will be noticed in another chapter. In the dimmer light of the old dispensation, God more frequently spoke to His people in this way. He specifically declared that He would make Himself known in a vision and speak in a dream (see Numbers 12:6).

In this way He spoke to Jacob in the dream of the ladder and the ascending and descending angels; to Joseph in the dream that foretold his bondage and his final prosperity; to Pharaoh's butler and baker in the dream that told of the exaltation of one and the execution of the other; to Solomon in the dream that promised him wisdom and all needful accessories; to Joseph in the dream which quieted his fears concerning Mary, the mother of our Lord, and also again in warning him to take the "young child" and flee for safety from Herod's murderous plot; to the wise men from the East warning them of the same danger;

to Pilate's wife warning her of the peril of persecuting Jesus; and to many others in just as marked a manner.

While there is no warrant in the words of Jesus for people to depend on dreams for guidance, it is evident that the Holy Spirit has, and sometimes does, speak to men through this agency. The abuse of dreams will be noticed further on.

Providences. The events of the moment are also often the wire on which good impressions come. God the Father delights through them to speak to His children. Opportunities to do good speak constantly with voices clear and strong. A death, an accident, a providential meeting, and kindred circumstances often impress with a sense of duty, and thus all things are made to work together for our good.

Over these and other wires which are laid between soul center and the divine mind, impressions are constantly coming.

IMPRESSIONS FROM BELOW

To drown good impressions, Satan has set up his kingdom, and exerts all of his ingenuity. He, too, has laid his telegraph lines and artfully operates them.

Satanic agency is a subject concerning which little is said, and yet by its subtle might millions have been and are being drawn into sin, despair, and final ruin; and millions more have been perplexed, and God's life plan for them greatly hindered or completely thwarted.

God's Word repeatedly recognizes the personality, ability, rank, influence, and plans of the devil. He loves to deceive people into the belief that he does not exist, as he knows people will not be on their guard against a foe in whose being they do not believe. Any who have thus been misled by him should be awakened by the manifold declarations

12

of the Word as to his personality, power, and plans.

It is divinely revealed that Satan was cast out of heaven; that he was cast down to hell; that he is the author of the fall; that he tempted Jesus; that he perverts the Scripture; that he opposes God's work; that he works lying wonders; that he appears as an angel of light; that he blinds, deceives, ensnares, and troubles the wicked; that he tempts, and that he afflicts and resists the saints. The Word also tells of Christ's victory over him by resisting his temptations, casting out his subordinates, destroying his works, rescuing his victims, defeating his conspiracy, conquering death, and banishing him and his followers forever from the presence of God and the glory of His power.

God's Word minutely and vividly presents his character as presumptuous, proud, powerful, wicked, malignant, subtle, deceitful, fierce, and cruel. He is compared to a "fowler," a "sower of tares," a "wolf," a "roaring lion," and a "serpent." He is called by over thirty different names descriptive of the different phases of his diabolical character. Among them are the following: "Murderer," "Dragon," "Father of Lies," "Old Serpent," "Wicked One," "Liar," and "Prince of the Devils." "The Accuser of the Brethren" is another of the names by which he is known in Scripture. In this character he has wrought much mischief. He accuses God's children:

To themselves: (1) by bringing wicked thoughts to their minds and then accusing them of thinking them. At such times we must remember that while we can not hinder such thoughts from coming, yet we can refuse to harbor them and thus remain guiltless; (2) by telling them when they are "in heaviness through manifold temptations" that because of this they have no religion at all; (3) by sorely tempting them and then making them believe that the temptation itself, instead of the yielding to it, is sin;

(4) by telling young converts, when they feel the movings of inbred sin still remaining in them, that because of this they never were truly converted; and (5) by suggesting to mature Christians that they have lost the blessing of perfect love simply because their emotions have in a measure subsided.

To each other: (1) by putting a bad construction to acts that are susceptible of a good one; (2) by charging wrong motives when the real motive is not known; (3) by telling one that he is not appreciated by others, or that he is slighted by them; and (4) by telling one that others have no religion at all because they do not in all things see eye to eye with him.

To the unconverted: (1) by telling them that Christians are deceived and that Christ is a hard master; (2) that soul-winners seek not them but their money; and (3) that church members are all hypocrites.

In these and other ways he seeks to perplex and sow discord. His might so marvelous, and strategic maneuvers so successful, turned earth that was designed for Eden into a habitation of cruelty and sepulcher of the dead.

He is the author, directly or indirectly, of all impressions from below. Many impressions come from him directly. They frequently are shot by him into the mind, like the leaping of lightning from a dark thundercloud, and astound by their suddenness and awfulness.

Evil angels. In Hannah W. Smith's *The Christian's Secret of a Happy Life* we read that "there are the voices of evil and deceiving spirits, who lie in wait to entrap every traveler entering these higher regions of spiritual life. In the same epistle which tells us that we are seated in heavenly places in Christ, we are also told that we shall have to fight with spiritual enemies. These spiritual enemies, whoever or whatever they may be, must necessarily communicate with us by means of our spiritual faculties and their voices, as the voice of God, are an inward impression made upon our spirit. Therefore, just as the Holy Spirit may tell us by impressions what the will of God is concerning us, so also will these spiritual enemies tell us by impressions what is their will concerning us, though not, of course, giving it their name."

"I believe," says John Wesley, "that united under Satan, they either range the upper regions, whence they are called princes of the power of the air, or, like him, walk about the earth as 'roaring lions seeking whom they may devour.'" A greater man than Wesley has said: "For we wrestle not against flesh and blood, but against principalities, against powers, against the rulers of the darkness of this world, against spiritual wickedness [wicked spirits] in high places" (Ephesians 6:12).

As good angels may be the messengers of impressions from above, so may evil ones, who are ever ready to blight and annoy and perplex and destroy, be of those from below.

Human influence. Bad people are wires over which evil impressions fly thick and fast. An evil word or glance may make an impression that is lasting.

When possible, Satan, too, is shrewd to get good people to carry his messages. He always does this when he can, as it helps to hide his purpose. Universalism is the most baneful kind of infidelity, because its messages are carried by men who profess to be ministers of Jesus. License of liquor could not live for a year were it not that the devil has secured for its defenders professedly good men. When men who are really good are deceived by Satan, and really think his messages are from above, the deception is deeper, and the danger still more dire.

The prayers of mistaken people. The influence of mind over mind is astonishing. If a person of strong will determines a certain thing in regard to another, and persistently insists upon it, there is reason to believe that the other person will feel the influence thereof, though thousands of miles away. Where a number of persons thus unite, the influence felt will be still stronger, and it will be felt whether the people are in the right or wrong.

The "one accord," which is essential for a church to prevail in prayer, embraces this principle. It is a power for good when in God's order; but when through ignorance or wrong motives it is not of the Spirit, it works perplexity and harm.

I know of a lady who has been tormented for over two years from this source. A good man, a minister of the Gospel, became possessed of the idea that she should marry him. He said that God had revealed it to him. The woman was fully saved, and felt just as sure that God had revealed the contrary to her. He commenced praying that God would show her her error, and while her convictions kept deepening that he was mistaken, yet often a disagreeable feeling would come to her as a result of his persistent, misguided prayer.

A person with weaker convictions of duty might have been led to yield to such an influence; but being enabled to see through it all as a design of Satan, she simply suffered the perplexity, and remained firm.

Satan delights to get good folks to waste their prayers over what is not the mind of the Spirit, as it diverts from God-given work.

These impressions seek to pull one out of the path of duty, and as they come through the medium of at least professedly good people they are sometimes very perplexing.

The flesh. Its appetites often clamor for unlawful indulgence, and cry so loud as to drown all other voices.

Self. The unrenewed and unsanctified "I" within always wants its own way, and will persistently plead for it. When messages from below harmonize with it, it is quick to carry them.

Bad reading. Its influence for evil cannot be estimated. Its impression for wrong will be as deep and lasting as hell itself.

These, and other wires, are shrewdly manipulated by Satan, and over them impressions are constantly reaching the mind. Their constant clicking is confusing and frequently confounding to those who have not the spiritual education to distinguish the sources from which they come.

The human soul beneath these influences is like a place where two winds meet, the cold blizzards from the frigid zones of satanic temptation and the refreshing gales from heavenly heights; or where two armies meet in fierce and deadly fray.

The soul itself can decide which shall prevail, and upon its decision hangs its character and its destiny. He who sides with convictions from above shall wear a victor's crown forever; with impressions from below shall be crownless and Christless through all eternity.

Be not deceived.

LUKE 21:8

Impressions from Below: Satan's Deceptions

As has been seen, Satan and his emissaries, disguised as "angels of light," by wrong impressions are ever seeking to ruin souls, and to divert God's children from their divinely appointed mission. He always shapes his methods to his victims, and whom he cannot openly allure he seeks to subtly deceive. He accomplishes his purpose, and men are betrayed.

Hence, we find that as a pan of meal which is prepared with poison appears precisely as one which is free from it, and would pass as harmless unless analyzed, so impressions from below may be apparent counterparts of those from above. They may exactly resemble them in the following important particulars:

They are inward impressions made upon our spirits.

They are often very strong impressions. Fanaticism is born in the land of strong but wrong impressions.

They occur repeatedly. See how Satan persisted with our first parents, with Job, and with Jesus. He will keep repeating his messages as long as he can deceive his victims into giving him a hearing, and all of his agents are possessed of like perseverance.

They frequently occur during prayer and other devotions.

Nothing is more in keeping with their object than to divert from communion with God, hence the idea that impressions are of God simply because they occur at such times is erroneous. They may be from Him and they may be from below.

Like good impressions, they may be brought to us by our friends. Job had more trouble from his friends than from both affliction and Satan combined. Though they meant well, the impressions they made were not from above. Eliphaz, Bildad, and Zophar, Job's misguided counselors, have had their counterparts in all ages.

Wrong impressions, like good ones, may be attended by a chain of circumstances which seem to confirm their truthfulness. Satan is allowed great latitude, and shows great cunning in arranging his program to thwart divine purposes. Selfish human nature also is eagle-eyed to claim as providential indications that were never so designed. It might have seemed providential to the assassin Booth that Lincoln was at the theater that fatal night, but does that prove that the murderer's impressions were of God?

Wrong impressions may be, and sometimes are, in harmony with our natural desires. The forbidden fruit which was proffered in paradise, and which appeared so "good" and "pleasant" and "desirable," has lost none of its attractiveness, and is far from being exhausted.

Evil impressions may also, like the good, be attended by striking passages of Scripture, which seem to sanction them. The devil and his agents, as in the temptation of Jesus, never fail to quote Scripture when they can pervert it to deceive and to strengthen their purposes. Mrs. H. W. Smith says she knew an earnest Christian who had the text, "All things are yours," so strongly impressed upon her mind in regard to some money that belonged to another person, that she felt that it was a direct command to steal the money, and after a struggle did so, with most grievous results. Like those from above, evil impressions may come suddenly and unexpectedly.

"Soon after receiving the blessing of perfect love," writes a correspondent, "I came across a man who had lost the experience because he had refused to yield to a sudden impression to kneel and pray when he entered a railroad car. I determined to be warned by what I thought was his mistake, but was led into a similar one in the following way: At the Des Moines Holiness Camp meeting I was walking one morning by the tabernacle when suddenly and strongly I was impressed to kneel down right where I was. Hesitating and embarrassed, I did so, though feeling very much out of place. After I yielded to this impulse, Satan made me believe I had better go through with it; I continued kneeling for some time. I arose wiser and determined not to be deceived by Satan in that manner any more."

In all of the above and in other particulars, impressions from below may be like those from above, and thus robed as "angels of light." Satan seeks through them to "deceive, if it were possible, the very elect."

On the enemy's success in passing this counterfeit coin, Dr. G. D. Watson says: "He doesn't work among sinners as he does among saints. He has one method of work among sinners, another for converted people, and another for sanctified people, and in the higher ranges of Christian life it is to imitate the Holy Spirit.

"Another trick of the devil is to get sanctified people where they are led by impressions. Some are frightened right off and go down; but if the devil finds he cannot scare you, and cannot make you stop testifying, then he will go around and attack you on the other side. I don't know whether you folks will believe what I am going to tell you, but it is the truth. The devil can make people feel tremendously happy. I have learned a great deal in the past fifteen years of the experiences of people. He can produce a fictitious happiness, and he will make you feel so with special reference to getting you to where you live on impressions, and then the devil has got all he wants. Then he puts on his Sunday clothes and turns himself into an angel of light.

"People—even Christian people—do not believe Scripture at this point. I have seen people so deluded by the devil, and I have said, 'Don't you know the devil can turn himself into an angel of light?'

" 'Oh, yes,' they say, 'but the devil isn't leading me! If God tells me to do so, I will do it.'

"Again he says, 'I am the Holy Ghost.' And you cannot detect him unless God helps you. He will begin by making you do something that is very nice for God. For instance, he will make you pray, but he will make you pray in the wrong way and at the wrong time. He will tell you to do a great many things, but he will always tell you, or impress you to do these things in a queer, outlandish, or unnatural way. He says to one sister, when the child is crying and the bread about to burn, 'Now, the Holy Ghost says you must go and pray an hour; let the baby cry and the coffeepot boil over.' I know these are facts. And the person goes off as sincere as an angel, and kneels down and prays; and the baby may get scalded to death.

"God the Holy Ghost, in all His leadings, never leads people in an abnormal way, or in an unnatural or strained way. God doesn't strain you; He doesn't put the thumbscrew on you, and strain your muscles until they crack and snap, but the devil does.

"A person goes to a meeting and says, 'The Lord sent me here today with a special message.' It may be time for the meeting to close, but he thinks he has a special message from the Lord, and he must tell it, though everybody else thinks it is time to go home. Those people insist that the Holy Ghost sent them. Now, it is nothing in the world but the devil. Why? Because the devil has got them on that road, going by impressions, going the way they feel. One man says, 'God has sanctified me and I want to prove to you that I am a holy man, and the Holy Ghost tells me to go down to the door, and have you walk over my body.' I am giving facts; all these things occurred. And they walked out of the door over his body to prove he was holy.

"The devil knows he cannot make us lie or steal, or do any of these things, but he is trying to make us do pious things in a most outlandish and most unnatural and most abnormal way. I tell you, there is a tremendous amount of that work done. People think they are led by the Holy Ghost, and they are led by the devil as an angel of light.

"You can recognize these people. In their prayers, in their sermons, in their efforts, there is always a sense of strangeness. They seem to be oppressed, to be burdened, to be unnatural. There is not tranquility or frankness. The devil is a hard master.

"Another trick of the devil is to imitate the Holy Ghost. The devil knows that the Holy Ghost is our leader. Jesus has gone to heaven. We have the written Word, but the Holy Ghost must explain to us the Word of God and reveal to us Jesus. And if the devil can imitate the Holy Ghost, that is his strength among Christian people. Among his own people he talks his own language.

"Another method of the devil is to imitate the Holy Spirit by giving people fictitious calls, fictitious beliefs, and dreams. The devil can make impressions and produce artificial happiness and artificial joy in order to switch off the soul. Of course, after he gets the soul off he will then make him do something more and more absurd, and by and by make him commit some sin; but he always begins delicately and tenderly. If a person is perfectly true to God, although the Lord may allow him to be annoyed and sometimes hindered by Satan, I cannot see but what God will make sure that his soul is delivered from the devil's power."

Thus artful is the approach of Satan toward the souls whom he seeks to betray. How needful, therefore, the admonition: "Finally, my brethren, be strong in the Lord, and in the power of his might. Put on the whole armour of God, that ye may be able to stand against the wiles of the devil. For we wrestle not against flesh and blood, but against principalities, against powers, against the rulers of the darkness of this world, against spiritual wickedness in high places. Wherefore take unto you the whole armour of God, that ye may be able to withstand in the evil day, and having done all, to stand" (Ephesians 6:10-13).

*Watch and pray,
that ye enter not
into temptation.*

MATTHEW 26:41

Impressions from Below: Satan's Judges

Preceding chapters have noticed that impressions come through many different agencies, and that there is often a striking resemblance between those from above and those from below.

Many impressions are so evidently from God that they need no testing, but all that are in any way doubtful should be summoned before a court of final appeal, the mention of which will soon be made.

Knowing that the person who will follow all impressions without stopping to test them will soon be at his mercy, Satan first of all seeks to ensnare by leading people to act at once without applying any test whatever. Then he will impress to do needless, unwise, untimely, and ridiculous things, and seek to deceive his subjects into believing that the promptings came from God. There is not one instance in the New Testament where the Spirit led a person to do an outlandish thing. God doesn't lead in that way.

Yielding to this influence, it is said that a young minister was strongly impressed when he entered a certain town that there he would find the woman who was to be his wife, and that on the street his attention was one day strongly drawn toward a lady whom the Spirit, he felt, revealed to him as that person. Imagine his chagrin when he saw her face to find that she was quite unattractive to him. This changed his impression. Had she been a beauty and rich, he might have taken it as divine.

Others are impressed to talk to everyone they meet, under all circumstances, about their souls. Some feel impressed to jump up and down and scream in meetings; others to lie down and let people walk over them to prove their humility; and at once putting these impressions in practice, they become the victims of Satan's wiles.

Saddest of all, the devil often succeeds in making people believe that these impressions are from above, and that they will resist the Spirit and backslide if they do not follow them. By this method he would keep those who will not do known sin, running on fruitless and often foolish errands.

There lies before me now a piteous appeal for spiritual help from a person who was in the experience of perfect love when she was strongly impressed to do a doubtful thing. She refused. Then Satan told her that she had quenched the Spirit and committed the unpardonable sin, and there was no hope for her. She believed this satanic impression, and sank down to the depths of unutterable anguish and despair, from which only Christ could lift her.

Frightful and many are the mistakes and disasters which have come from being led by untried impressions. To keep from the discriminating light of the detecting proof tests which God has provided, Satan has devised many ingenious and deceptive expedients. As the rightful judges never will render a decision in his favor, but always detect the slightest error, he makes a desperate effort to prevail upon persons to appeal to other judges whom he can bribe to decide as he wishes. If possible, he will push people to act upon doubtful impressions without trying them at all; but if they will "try the spirits whether they are of God," then he insists that they shall be tried before a court of his dictation. The following are among the judges which he recommends, and which have betrayed multitudes:

Feelings. People who are duped by this judge follow their feelings instead of their convictions. Impressions which harmonize with their feelings are fondled, and other impressions are given a cold reception. If their feelings are crossed they raise such a cry as to drown the whisperings of the still, small voice within, and then seek their selfish gratification. They sometimes do very unscriptural things because they "feel like it," and for the same reason avoid the cross and the self-denial which it imposes. They mistake the voice of their own feelings for a message from above, and, following the decisions of this judge, they are betrayed into wrong action. Well did Wesley exhort his followers to "trample under foot the enthusiastic doctrine that we are to do good only when we feel like it." He who tests his convictions by his feelings, instead of God's judges, is as foolish as a man who would take his case out of a wise and righteous court and put it in the power of a crying child.

Imagination. Fancy is often quick to seize an impression, paint it, and make it appear as real and beautiful as a blooming rose. The Christian, of course, renounces all imaginations that are known to be wrong; but in order to divert from the work and the life-plan which God has marked out, imagination will often paint another work and point to another plan which some wrong impression has suggested, and thus seek to lead from the path where duty calls.

A person sometimes has an impression that he ought to have a certain desirable appointment. In fact, a number often feel "strongly impressed" that they should have the same place. Then they imagine themselves there, and

when the appointments are made and their fancy bubble
bursts, they weep like children because the voice of their
imaginations did not prove to be the voice of God.
Sometimes imagination takes foreboding of evil and makes
it seem as real as fact, and goads to worry over what
never comes.

Every "imagination" that does not stand the tests above
mentioned should be "cast down." He who substitutes it
instead of them will find himself in as sad a plight as
the student who might seek to make a paintbrush light his
room instead of lighting a candle. The burden of Jeremiah's
message against God's people was that they followed
"their own imaginations" instead of heeding the divine
voice.

Who is there that has not sometimes had a "strong
impression" that an absent friend was sick, or in danger,
or dying, and afterward found that it was all imagination?
The devil is called the "tormentor," and he loves to tantalize
by this or any other means.

"Beware," wrote Wesley, "of a heated imagination. . . .
Some charge their own imaginations on the will of God,
and that not written but impressed on their hearts. If
these impressions be received as a rule of action instead of
the written Word, I know nothing so wicked or absurd
but that we may fall into, and that without remedy."

Chance texts. The habit of turning to some chance text
and hinging action upon that, has prevailed with some.
This is as if a physician should prescribe for his patient by
opening his books at random and writing down the first
medicine which catches his eye! Or as if a lawyer would
open a book of legal lore and give his client the chance
counsel which he thus might find! Is spiritual indolence or
ignorance more pardonable than medical or legal?

The come-outer is impressed that he should leave the
church. He urges the divinity of his impression by taking

30

as a test the first text which meets his eye as he opens the Bible. It chances to be, "Come out from among them, and be ye separate." With this text Satan blinds his eyes to the whole teaching of Scripture in regard to the organized church, and on it he drifts down the stream of "come-outism," over the falls of fanaticism.

Another person is impressed that women ought not to do public work. He opens his Bible, and by chance his eye catches, "Let the woman learn in silence." The whole question is settled in an instant! And so easily, too! And thus wresting this Scripture from its proper place, he peacefully pillows his head upon it, and lies down on the railroad track of the facts of Scripture, right and sense in the matter, and is crushed by the wheels of truth. "Search the Scriptures," not "fool" with them, is the divine command.

Dreams. God has spoken to men by dreams, but this is not His usual way. There is, under the Spirit's dispensation, no Scripture warrant for depending upon them for guidance. Jeremiah called them "chaff" when compared to the revealed Word. He who substitutes the chaff of dreams for the wheat of Bible truth will soon become spiritually starved. Many people have allowed themselves to be alarmed because previous impressions were strengthened by dreams which were merely born of bad digestion. The Bible speaks of "false dreams" and "filthy dreamers," and complains of those who caused the people to forget God by "their dreams which they tell every man to his neighbour."

A certain person received me very coldly where I was once engaged in revival work because of a striking dream he had had of an evangelist which he thought referred to me. Before the meeting closed he changed his mind, and thought it must have meant some other person.

A Christian lady, after losing her husband, dreamed that

a relative came to her home and brought a man, and said to her, "I have brought you this man for your husband." The dream made a very deep impression, and the features of the promised husband were vividly fixed in her mind. She actually expected the fulfillment of the dream, but looked for it in vain to the day of her death.

All impressions made by dreams which do not meet the approval of the rightful tests should be allowed to vanish. To follow them may prove as fatal as for an engineer, because of "a strong impression made by a dream," to run his train without orders from headquarters. In either case, fearful wreckage may be the result.

Wesley wisely warns, "Do not hastily ascribe things to God. Do not easily suppose dreams, voices, impressions, visions, or revelations to be from God. They may be from Him. They may be from nature. They may be from the devil. Therefore believe not every spirit, but 'try the spirits, whether they be from God.' "

Infatuation. Under the magic charms of this enchantress, all voices but her own are but faintly heard or altogether hushed. Her victims are restive under any restraint that crosses her whims, and they frequently at her impetuous behests do violence to sacred vows and teachings of the Word divine. The still, small voice of duty is no more their delight, but the wine she offers intoxicates with pleasure. Too late they learn that beneath its sparkling surface there lurks disappointment, chagrin, and frequently disgrace and even death. Satan may make people think that the voice of their infatuation is the voice of the Holy Ghost.

Under its seductive sway it is said that three young men went in succession to their spiritual adviser, and each claimed that he was strongly "impressed of God" that he should marry a certain attractive woman of wealth. One individual felt sure that God had revealed to him that he should marry a woman who was already the promised wife of another person. Another Christian man broke a long engagement and married the object of his infatuation. The woman whom he thus had wronged died soon after, and the lightnings of God's judgments have ever since been leaping upon the wrongdoer. Attachments thus are frequently fostered which lead to alienations, law suits, neighborhood and church divisions, sundered family circles, and sometimes suicide and murder. Similar instances to the above abound on every side. The ruin wrought by bad people and the ridiculous antics cut by some good people under the influence of this enchantress, show that it is foolish and often fatal to follow her decisions. To appeal to her is as unwise as it would be to put a giddy girl upon the judge's bench. Delighted is the devil when he can delude one to heed her siren voice instead of appealing to tests divine.

Impulse. Under this influence, impressions which are very strong are acted upon in haste, to be repented of at leisure. God never hurries people to do doubtful things. The devil does. Thus influenced, impulsive Peter drew his sword and made it needful for Jesus to perform the miracle of healing a sundered ear. Modern Peters by similar acts are constantly making miracles necessary to counteract the harm they have done. "He that believeth shall not make haste" applies to all action concerning the righteousness of which the child of God has any doubt.

Passion. Many have attributed impressions to come from God which were born of no other parentage than their own rebellious passions. Saul of Tarsus, beneath the sway of this power, "breathing out slaughter" against the followers of Jesus, tells us that he verily thought he was doing God service. It is sometimes miscalled "righteous indignation," but loses none of the lionlike in its nature by the lambskin in which it thus is robed. Beware of its decision. Impulse and passion often prove a Niagara which drowns the voice of duty, and sweeps thousands of victims over the falls of irretrievable loss.

Prejudices and preconceived notions. These, by their hue and cry, attempt to deafen the ear to every voice which does not agree with them. Peter, though fully sanctified, had to be taken aside and given a special object lesson before he could distinguish, above the din of these two voices, the Spirit's call to preach the Gospel to the Gentiles. These two arbiters always interpret impressions according to their own views, and it is folly to appeal to them. Yet they are misleading millions. I have known their victims to be shocked at new and successful measures which the Holy Ghost would suggest in revival work, simply because these two censors were offended.

The flesh. The voices of the body often clamor for excessive and unlawful gratification. Any impression which gives them license is popular with them. They are all ambitious to sit upon the throne of the soul and control its decisions, and must be "kept under," or instead of the "fruits of the Spirit," there will be the "lusts of the flesh," a harvest of thistles.

The opinions of other people. There is a sense in which "in the multitude of counsellors there is safety," but more frequently there is confusion. He who seeks counsel from others more than from God will soon find discordant human voices drowning the inner voice, and know the truthfulness of the declaration that "cursed be the man that trusteth in man, and maketh flesh his arm." God often leads His children contrary to the counsels of their best friends, to teach them to rely on Him. So the voices of even our best friends cannot be substituted for the tests which will be named. Satan, or self, will sometimes originate a very strong impression in the mind of Brother Impulse and Brother Self-confidence, and make them believe it is of the Lord. It may relate to the action of

34

Brother Tender Conscience. With the solemnity and dogmatic certainty of an infallible oracle, they inform him of the revelation which they claim to have gotten of God, implying that they doubt his decision, and, perhaps, piety, if he does not accept their message as divine. I have known persons to bring and urge such messages, when to follow them would be to violate conscience, common sense, and the clearest teachings of the Word.

Signs. Satan can easily counterfeit signs, as he did with Moses in Egypt. It is evident that signs would be an unsafe standard by which to try impressions. It is perilous to depend upon them. Yet the whole Simple family frequently does it. If they have an impression that one of their family is not to live long, and a bird flies into the room, or a mirror is broken, they are alarmed. They think it a sure sign of further mortality if a grave caves in or if it rains upon the coffin on its way to its last long home. They are sure it is a bad sign to begin a job on Friday, and are governed by many similar superstitions. It is also believed that some people who don't like to be classed with the Simple family are affected by such signs to a greater degree than they are free to confess.

Chance happenings. Another trick of the adversary to get people to avoid rightful tests of impressions, is to prevail upon them to submit them to some chance happening. Brother and Sister Truth-seeker have often been led astray in this way. They are impressed to do a certain thing, and decide that if the sun rises clear they will do it, if cloudy, not. If a certain chance event occurs they will take an impression to be of God; if it does not occur, not of Him. It might fittingly be called "religious gambling." It is a sort of "penny toss" arrangement which finds no sanction since the Holy Ghost fell at Pentecost. That good people have sometimes resorted to it simply proves their infirmity. It was before Pentecost that the apostles "cast lots" in electing a successor of Judas. Had they waited until after, they doubtless would have taken a different course, and been saved the mortification of choosing a man who never was heard of afterward, and of forestalling the Spirit, who put Paul in the place of Judas.

Two persons had kept company for a long time and were to have been married. The man finally became enamored of another person and felt "strongly impressed" to marry her. He went to his pastor for advice, but as it did not agree with his desires, he decided to settle the matter by this device of the devil. The lot fell in favor of his new infatuation, and he followed it with results that eternity will tell. A judge who would toss a penny to decide a case instead of weighing the evidence and determining thereby would be thought insane; yet the Christian who tampers in this way with life's decisions is no more wise. God's tests, if questioned a thousand times, always respond with the same reply, but this chance device, if repeatedly appealed to, always contradicts itself, thus proving its satanic sonship.

Its use drives to wrong conclusions, dwarfs reason, fosters ignorance, offers incense to chance, perplexes the conscience, pleases Satan, and grieves the Holy Ghost.

These, and other similar devices, are often used by "the world, the flesh, and the devil," to accomplish their designs. The deception practiced is often so subtle as to escape detection only from those who have learned to try them by divine tests. While Satan is allowed great latitude in his efforts to deceive, yet he can go no further than God permits.

It would not be surprising if there are ways revealed whereby all his counterfeit coins can be detected, and God's voice always be clearly and unmistakably known. Given a God with whom all things are possible, a Savior whose mission is to "destroy the works of the devil" and who has promised His children "power . . . over all the power of the enemy," such a provision may be confidently looked for.

But they rebelled,
and vexed his Holy Spirit:
therefore he was turned
to be their enemy,
and he fought against
them.

ISAIAH 63:10

Impressions from Below: Results of Following Them

When people act on every sudden and strong or repeated impression, instead of "pondering their paths" and submitting to the tests which will determine their character, sad results follow. The following are some of them:

Perplexity. Many have been perplexed and bewildered and driven to the very verge of insanity in this way.

The devil comes with a suggestion. He clothes it in robes of light so that it appears to be the truth. He persistently pushes it. If resisted, he claims that those who do so are resisting the Spirit. If they yield to it, he then tears off his "robe of light" and laughs at their deception. He says, "No harm," when he seeks to allure astray, and afterward accuses with fierce fury, a foretaste of the taunts with which he will tantalize the lost throughout eternity.

A student was tempted to leave school and engage in revival work. The proposal came unexpectedly, and he was pushed to a decision. He loved that work, and without reflection agreed to go. But this decision filled him with dissatisfaction, and as he prayed about it the Spirit took the providences connected with his coming to school and remaining there, and showed him that God's leadings still were schoolward. As he was released from his hasty promise, his perplexity vanished, and the sunshine of God's favor again beamed upon him.

Unwise action. Every act that is not in harmony with God's will is unwise. He who acts hurriedly upon impulses is frequently betrayed into such action.

A friend of mine was just cheated out of one hundred dollars in this way. A man called upon him, told a pitiful story, and so presented his case as to work upon his sympathies. He finally requested a loan of one hundred dollars. My friend had spoken to him about his soul; feared a refusal might harden him toward Christians, and out of his impulsive, generous heart lent him the money. The next week the man deserted his family, and left the country with quite a sum of money that he had secured in a similar way. Had my friend reflected, prayed, and talked the matter over with his wife, and taken time to have applied the tests, he would have saved his money, the mortification of being deceived, and the wrong of thus bidding a thief "Godspeed."

Disappointment. Most failures in business doubtless come because God's guidance is not sought and followed. Failures in religious work may result from the same cause. Revival meetings which are projected for the sake of personal aggrandizement, or simply through sectarian zeal and rivalry, are doomed for this reason. I knew of a minister who held a series of meetings in a certain place chiefly to keep out another denomination. He was not led by God, and his efforts ended in disappointment. God will have His children learn to let Him lead, and if the lesson costs them a thousand disappointments, it is better than that it should go unlearned.

Salvation hindered. Neglect to follow where and when the Spirit leads often greatly hinders the work of salvation. This is forcibly illustrated by the following incident from the pen of one of the readers of *God's Revivalist*: "At one Sabbath evening service I noticed, with some surprise, a man occupying a seat at my right. It was an old acquaintance, who had at one time lived in our home. I was surprised, because, though living near the church, I had never before seen him in any place of public worship. I knew him to be one of those men who pride themselves upon their morality, and think that they need no other salvation, and who are perfectly indifferent to all the claims of God.

"There he sat, listening with the closest attention. Suddenly it was suggested to my mind that I should, at the close of the service, seek this man out and invite him to Jesus. I was startled, and began to question with myself the impropriety and the uselessness of such a proceeding. But the impression deepened until the pressure upon my nerves became so great that I could scarcely arise from my seat. I decided to speak if opportunity presented. Soon Mr. P., seeing me in the congregation, came at once to where I was standing, and after making inquiries about my family, stood for a few moments in silence as if waiting for me to speak, but my courage failed, and soon he left with the crowd and the opportunity was lost.

"I sought my home in tears, and passed a sleepless night. For many days I could not unburden my heart of its load. I tried to make myself believe that, perhaps, after all, the impression was not from the Lord. He was pleased to place the assurance that it was beyond the possibility of a doubt. It was in this wise: I saw Mr. P. coming up the walk to my door one afternoon, and instantly resolved to put the matter to a test. He came in, and greeting me in his usual bright and genial manner, remarked pleasantly, that, as he chanced to be passing, he thought he would drop in and see how we were prospering. I saw at once

41

that whatever might have been the state of his mind on that memorable Sabbath evening, he was quite different now.

"In a few minutes I had told him of my convictions of duty, of my cowardly shrinking, and my subsequent remorse, sparing myself in nothing. While I was speaking in hurried and trembling tones, a wave of feeling rushed over his face which, as it receded, left him very pale. After a few moments of silence he remarked in a constrained voice, as though it cost him much to speak, 'I feel that I owe it to you, Mrs. N., to be as frank with you as you have been with me, so I will say, that previous to that meeting, I had been for many weeks strangely conscious in my heart of my neglect of duty to God, to my family and to my fellowmen.

" 'I was brought to look upon life and its responsibilities as I had never done before, though I scarcely knew what it all meant, for I found my mind so dark and ignorant about these things, and that evening, after a day of unusual depression, I turned my step in the direction of the church, with no intention but to get away for a little time from my own company. Once there, the singing, the Scripture lesson, and the prayer affected me as nothing of the kind had ever done before; and the sermon, every word of it, burned itself into my soul till I was ready to cry out in anguish. I saw myself a lost sinner, and resolved, if opportunity offered, to confess my convictions and solicit the help of Christians.

" 'The meeting closed, but no one approached me on that subject, and looking wistfully about me I saw you, and instantly the remembrance of the family altar in your home, at which I had knelt out of respect to your family in other days, came rushing to my mind, and catching at the last straw of hope I came to your side. I did not blame you at the time for not speaking, nor do I now, for how could you know that I should care to converse on these things, indifferent as I have always been? I went out of that house in bitterness of spirit, saying to myself, "Well, there cannot be much in Christianity after all, if among so many of its adherents as were present tonight, not one could be found that cares whether a poor sinner is saved or lost. If that is being Christlike it is different from what I supposed, and I will dismiss this whole matter from my mind and take the risk of passing as well as the rest." From that moment I have had no feeling on the subject, and yet I am conscious of a different feeling, a bitter and defiant one.

" 'I would never have mentioned this to anyone had you not spoken as you did, but if I were you, I think I would follow up such impressions—pardon the suggestion—for you do not know how much good might result.'

"He must have noticed the anguish in my face, for he added kindly, 'Do not trouble yourself about this circumstance. I dare say it will be all right with me in the end, but if it is not, you are not to blame.' But I could not think so. I could not dispossess my mind of the idea that if this man were lost, his blood would be required at my hand. It was a heavy burden, and one that was ever present with me, and even after Mr. P.'s conversion, several years later, I could not think of it without pain and remorse, nor can I yet. But it has taught me a lesson, which, perhaps, nothing else could have done.

"God cannot trust His work to disobedient ones; but to the obedient and faithful He will give blessed opportunities for soul-winning, and great shall be their reward. Oh, that I could write one message with the point of a diamond upon the heart of every Christian. It should be this: Be sure that the slightest impression upon your heart disposing you to do Christian work has the divine stamp, and then obey at whatever cost."

43

Undue hurry. Such persons forget that "if the Holy Spirit inspires anything, He always gives time to consult upon it with God." Impetuous, and hurried by the pressure of self or satanic influence, they rush pell-mell in ways that are far more hurried than wise, and miss the guidance of the still, small voice that would have brought certainty and satisfaction.

Formality. It is to be feared that some, like the Jews who rejected Jesus, influenced by their pride, preconceived notions, and prejudices, have turned a deaf ear to divine guidance and quenched the Spirit; and, like them, kept up a mere formal worship, totally destitute of the life and power of heart piety. Substituting formality for Christianity, their condition is sad, and is one of the prevalent and pitiable results which flows from following "impressions from below."

Fanaticism. There is much more danger today of people perishing amid the icebergs of formality than in the wildfire of fanaticism. Both should be avoided. All fanaticism, from primitive times to the present, has come from discarding proper tests and following "impressions from below." This is one of the perils which threatens spiritual people just as a fast express train is more likely to leap the track than a slow train. God's trains, however, never need to leap over the chasm of fanaticism, and never will if they follow His instructions.

Despair. When Satan succeeds in deceiving a soul to do or not do, as the case may be, he often sweeps down on it like a cyclone, and accuses it of committing the "unpardonable sin." He quotes Hebrews 10:26, 27 in regard to "willful sin" and its penalty; also 2 Peter 2:20, 21 about the "latter end [being] worse with them than the beginning"; and Hebrews 6:4-6, about it being "impossible" for some "if they shall fall away, to renew them again to repentance," and kindred passages. He blindfolds the eyes of his victims to the bountiful provision of pardon to the penitent, and with vehemence and persistence brings such Scripture as the above to their minds. Unless they fly to the blood and claim victory in Jesus, they become the victims of great despair.

The following letter vividly illustrates this power of Satan at this point: "I hope that you will let my urgent need of 'help in time of trouble' prove sufficient apology for appealing to you, an entire stranger, for help in this, my greatest hour of need. I have just been reading the chapter entitled: 'Back from Babylon' from *Out of Egypt into Canaan*, and it has brought a faint ray of hope to a heart fettered with despair. I want to write you, and beg you to help me. Three months ago I entered into the Canaan of perfect love. Now I am the most miserable being in existence. I believe it all came from resisting an impression from the Spirit. I was not sure it was from God, and for fear it would lead me into fanaticism, resisted, and after a time my joy and peace departed. I yielded then, but it seemed too late. The most awful feelings would take possession of me, and though in the daytime I could resist them with all the strength of my will, at night it seemed to me Satan took possession of my very will power, and now the most dreadful and rebellious thoughts rush through my heart, and I have no will to resist, no power to give them as I once did to Jesus to remove. Last week, after four sleepless nights with the constant agony of those awful temptations, I suddenly 'gave up my shield.' I thought I was already lost, and to try to dull the agony of the thought I tried to believe there was no Christ. I gave my sweet experience from God's Holy Spirit into the hands of the enemy, and though I would instantly have recalled it all, it is too late. I cannot tell you of the agony

45

in which I live. My dear mother is in heaven, and I, the oldest daughter, cannot confess to the dear father or the sweet young sisters who look ever to me for guidance, that I am a traitor. It would shake their faith forever. The conviction is in my soul that I have committed the 'unpardonable sin.' I try to pray, but think always of 'Esau who found no place for repentance, though he sought it carefully and with tears.' Since reading your book, I have been fasting and trying to lift my poor dead heart to the Lord. I find no relief, and so I write to you, and beg of you to grant me this request: As soon as you receive this, state my pitiful case to someone who is full of faith and the Holy Ghost, and 'agree touching your petition' with fasting. I feel as did the impotent man, and that I am led captive by the devil at his will. I have found it easy to ask you this; I believe you will grant my request. It is a soul out of its deepest need appealing to another. Please keep the pitiful secret of my name; but won't you write a few lines to one, once your sister in Christ?"

In the above instance, Satan evidently tempted to do some doubtful thing. Divinely led, she refused, and then he succeeded in making her believe that the impressions came from God instead of him, and that she had quenched the Spirit.

All such should remember that "if any man sin, we have an advocate with the Father," and that they who have committed the unpardonable sin are so hardened that it does not even trouble them.

All the fearful results that follow a refusal to be guided by God are too terrible to tell. The most vivid portrayal of them, perhaps, that can be found, is in the wilderness wanderings of the children of Israel after they refused to be led into the promised land. May we each so resist "impressions from below," and be so fully "led of the Spirit," that we will never have personally the experiences to which this chapter points, but may continually abide in the sunshine of His smile, in whose "presence is fulness of joy," and at whose right hand "there are pleasures for evermore."

Prove all things;
hold fast
that which is good.

1 THESSALONIANS 5:21

———————————

To the law and to the testimony:
if they speak not
according to this word,
it is because
there is no light in them.

ISAIAH 8:20

Impressions:
How to Test Them

God has made such ample provision for the guidance of
His children that they may be just as sure that they are led
by Him as that they are saved.

In order to do this it is needful to apply to every doubtful
impression certain detecting tests. To do this sometimes
requires keen spiritual sight, yet is a privilege which
the least of God's children may enjoy. "His sheep hear his
voice" and "follow him," and we would not be commanded
to "try the spirits whether they are of God," if there was
no danger from them, or if we were powerless to distinguish
them. All impressions which are from above bear the four
following distinguishing features. They are *scriptural*—
in harmony with God's will as revealed in His Word; *right*—
in harmony with God's will as revealed in man's moral
nature; *providential*—in harmony with God's will as revealed
in His providential dealings; and *reasonable*—in harmony
with God's will as revealed to a spiritually enlightened
judgment.

Many impressions are so evidently of God that they need
no testing, but all that are in any way doubtful should be
summoned before this infallible court of final appeal.

Every impression from above has upon it the divine

49

stamp: **SRPR**: **S**criptural, **R**ight, **P**rovidential, **R**easonable.
It is perilous to act on an impression which lacks any of
these letters.

Scriptural. Impressions from above are always in harmony
with the teaching of the Word. Other impressions may
wrest isolated passages to their support, but God's guidance
is in harmony with the whole blessed Book. It never leads
a person to do contrary to its teachings or to influence
others to such a course. On every doubtful point, the
question, "What does the Bible teach?" should lead to
search until that knowledge is gained, and then it should
be acted upon. While it is a book of general principles,
it also covers almost every practical point that ever occurs
in human life.

Multitudes of impressions from below die of fright at
their own images when they are compelled to look in the
mirror of God's Word. The Sword of the Spirit, which
is the Word of God, will pierce the thickest armor in which
Satan can mail his deceptive suggestions. Then let every
doubtful impression first of all be rigidly examined under
the focalized light of all that the Scripture teaches in
regard to it.

"It is a dangerous error," says Dougan Clark, "to neglect,
or reject, or ignore the teachings of the Holy Bible, on
the pretext that the inward teachings of the Spirit are more
valuable than the outward letter. It will always be found
that those who love God most love His Bible most. He who
is taught by Scripture is taught of the Lord; and it is
never by the Holy Spirit that anyone is induced to desert
the outward revelation written by holy men whom He
inspired. . . . If our heavenly Father has clearly revealed
His will by the written Word, in reference to any point, we
are not to expect another revelation from His Spirit to
teach us our duty in that regard."

Jesus Himself thus appealed to the Word when tempted

by Satan, and victorious are all His followers who walk in His steps.

Mormonism, the Oneida community, Universalism, and all their fraternity of erroneous doctrines which are born of impressions from below, yet claim to be of God, stand convicted of guilt by this infallible test.

In regard to every doubtful impression, ask: "Is it scriptural?" If it is not, then it should be transported as a felon to external exile in the Siberia of doomed impressions.

Right. God speaks through the voice of man's moral convictions. The rule of right and wrong in moral matters is universal. Even cannibals know that it is wrong to steal and lie and kill, "which show the work of the law written in their own hearts."

"Our own minds," wrote Charles Finney, "their convictions, their necessary affirmations, do truly reveal God and many of the great truths that respect our relation to Him and to His government."

Impressions which are from God are always right. They may be contrary to our feelings, our prejudices, and our natural inclinations, but they are always right. They will stand all tests, and their rightfulness soon becomes a conviction which cannot be shaken.

The voice of Scripture and of right always agree, but many who have not all the light of Scripture are convinced by the voice of this monitor within which way the path of duty lies. This voice brands as from below any impression which would lead to a wrong act.

Millions of impressions, if compelled to answer the simple question "Are you right?" will blush and hesitate and squirm, and finally in confusion retire.

Providential. God often speaks to His children through His providences. "In examining the Scriptures upon this matter," writes G. D. Watson, "we find that the peculiar sphere of the Father's leading is providence; the peculiar sphere of Christ's guidance is the written Word, and the peculiar sphere of the Spirit's guidance is direct conviction and illumination upon the heart and spiritual senses.

"The providence of God touches at every point our physical being and wants, and appeals to our common sense. The *logos*, the Word of God, takes hold of our immortal nature and appeals to our faith; the Holy Spirit operates immediately on our heart and mind, giving us such impellings and restrainings, such premonitions or drawings as compose the living, practical filling up on the outline of guidance."

Emphatic mention of this test of impressions is made by Upham in his valuable treatise on divine guidance: "The mind of God as it is disclosed in His providences, and the mind of the Holy Spirit as it reveals itself in the soul are one; and, consequently, in their different developments can never be at variance, but will always be at harmony with each other.

"They throw light, the one upon the other. Certain it is that the mind of the Spirit, in all cases of mere practical action and duty, cannot, as a general thing, be clearly and definitely ascertained except in connection with providential dispensations. Such dispensations are the outward light which throws a reflex illumination upon the inward light. And this is so general a law of the divine operation, that persons who are truly led by the Spirit of God are generally, and, perhaps, always, found to keep an open eye upon the divine providences, as important and true interpreters of the inward leadings. . . . As instruments of music will not give utterance to their beautiful sounds till they are touched and swept by an outward hand, so the inward inspiration of the Holy Ghost is to some extent latent in the mind, and is not susceptible of being distinctly analyzed in its responses to the spiritual ear until it receives its interpretation from the outward application of providential events.

"If a leading is of God, the 'way will always open for it.' The Lord assures us of this when He says, 'When he putteth forth his own sheep, he goeth before them, and the sheep follow him: for they know his voice.' Notice here the expressions, 'goeth before' and 'follow.' He goes before to open a way, and we are to follow in the way thus opened. It is never a sign of a divine leading when a Christian insists on opening his own way, and riding roughshod over all opposing things. If the Lord goes before us, He will open all doors to us, and we shall not need ourselves to hammer them down. The Word declares: 'Behold, I have set before thee an open door, and no man can shut it' " (quoted in *The Christian's Secret of a Happy Life*, by Hannah W. Smith).

This open door of providential opportunity awaits every person who follows impressions from above.

"I will go before thee," declares Jehovah, to all who follow Him, "and make the crooked places straight: I will break in pieces the gates of brass, and cut in sunder the bars of iron." Impressions from above find "crooked places" divinely straightened, gates of brass divinely broken, and bars of iron divinely sundered.

The providential openings which thus ever welcome those divinely led are marvelous. God never impresses a Noah to build an ark, or a Solomon a temple, but that means, material, and men await their approaching faith. He never impresses a Philip to go preach to an individual, but that He prepares the person for Philip's preaching. He never says to an imprisoned Peter, "arise quickly," but that Peter will find chains providentially broken, and gates providentially burst.

The Peters that are mourning because they cannot, on

account of providential hindrances, do what they claim God is impressing them to, are not being influenced by impressions from above. This third door to the secret chamber of certainty, in regard to being divinely led, always flies open as by magic before the face of him whom God is guiding.

God never prompts us to do impossibilities, therefore His leadings can always be followed. He who is impressed to do something which in the nature of the case he cannot do, may be sure that the leading is from some other source than above. Peter Dashaway is often humbled by the failure of his impressions to meet this simple test. If the way will not open for us to put our impressions in practice, and providential indications are all to the contrary, it is well to bury them. They may die hard, but death should be their doom.

We cannot forbear to quote further from the luminous teachings of G. D. Watson on this frequently puzzling point: "The Holy Ghost never guides us contrary to the Word. The Word never guides us contrary to Providence, and Providence does not guide us contrary to the Word or Spirit. So, these three elements of divine guidance are always harmonious.

"Some years ago a lady was at the altar seeking a clean heart. Satan was there, and in addition to all the other tests which he brought to her mind, for he may present tests on such occasions, was the following: She told my wife, 'There is one thing in my way. Something seemed to say to me, "Will you go to Africa?" '

"There have been more people that have had to 'go to Africa' than anywhere in this universe! I had to 'go to Africa.' We all have to 'go to Africa.' Everybody that has got sanctified for the last five years, almost, has had to 'go to Africa.'

" 'Well,' my wife said, 'let us see about it; you know God

does not ask anything foolish of you. Tell me your
circumstances.' She had a husband and four or five children
and a house to care for. Said my wife (who has more
common sense than I have), 'Do you think the Holy Ghost
will ask you to do a thing that God's providence wouldn't
allow? Will God's Spirit run against God's providence?
And do you think God will ask you to go off to Africa, and
leave your children and husband?' Well, she didn't see
how He could. Then said my wife, 'It may be that twenty
years from now God will want you in Africa, and God
may turn things so you can go. You just simply say, "Yes,
Lord, I will go when You send me," and settle it. All
God wants is your heart loyalty. God would rather have
your perfect heart loyalty than have Africa, or China,
or anything else.' She said, 'Yes, Lord, I will do anything
You say,' and she got through. That was the end of Africa.
When you want to be divinely led, simply consult God's
providence and consult God's Word and consult the
convictions of God's Spirit upon your heart, and the Lord,
if you are humble and teachable, will see that you are
properly led."

Reasonable. Impressions from above are always in
harmony with a spiritually enlightened judgment. God has
given us reasoning powers for a purpose, and He respects
them, appeals to them, and all of His leadings are in
unison with them. He will bring up all the facts in the
case in such a way as to convince that His leadings are all
in harmony with sanctified common sense. Indeed, when
the first three tests above mentioned are met, reason
can but accept the conclusions which they bring.

I have a friend who was frightened from receiving the
baptism of the Holy Spirit, because Satan kept suggesting
to her that if she did she would have to do absurd and
unreasonable things. He "impressed" her that she ought to
go and preach at a political meeting, talk religion to

everyone she met on the street and everywhere, and do
kindred unreasonable things. He made her believe that
these impressions came from God instead of him, and thus
fearfully perplexed her. Satan took the fact that we are to
do good "as we have opportunity," and with it sought
to compel her to force opportunities. An appeal to this test
would have defeated him. God never requires an
unreasonable thing. He invites us to "reason" with Him,
and appeals to our judgments that His service is a
"reasonable service."

As someone has said, it is a wise thing to "rap impressions
on the head and see if they have sound sense." If we, in
our finiteness, can see that they are unreasonable, the
conclusion is resistless that they cannot come from God.
In the following passage Upham says that we must not
depend on our unaided reasoning powers for this purpose,
but that God helps us to see the truth through their
use: "If we shut our natural eyes we will stumble over
many obstacles, and just so if we refuse to permit God to
illuminate our judgment, or ride recklessly forward over
its rightful decisions, we will come to trouble.

"God deals with us as with rational beings, and it is a
consequence of that recognition of our rationality that He
does not require us to act upon sudden suggestions or
impressions, even if they come from Himself without our
first subjecting them to the scrutiny of reason.

"Here it is that we find the ground of our safety in
respect to a method of operation upon us which otherwise
would be likely to be full of danger.

"Accordingly, when a sudden suggestion is presented to
the mind, we ought to delay upon it, although it may
seem, at first sight, to require immediate action.

"We should compare it with the will of God, as revealed
in the Bible.

"We should examine it dispassionately and deliberately,

with the best light of reason, and with the assistance of prayer.

"Indeed, if the suggestion comes from God, it is presented with this very object, not to lead us to action without judgment and without reason, but to arouse the judgment from its stupidity, and to put it upon a train of important inquiry. . . . This is a great practical and religious truth, however much it may be unknown in the experience of those who are not holy in heart; that the decision of a truly sanctified judgment is, and of necessity must be, the voice of God speaking in the soul."

John Wesley advised that all earthly considerations be scrutinized under the light of the Bible: "Try all things by the written Word, and let all bow down before it. You are in danger of enthusiasm [fanaticism] every hour, if you depart ever so little from Scripture; yea, or from the plain literal meaning of any text taken in connection with the context. And so you are if you despise or lightly esteem reason, knowledge, or human learning, every one of which is an excellent gift of God, and may serve the noblest purposes."

The Holy Spirit is our divinely appointed guide. We are to be led by Him. He speaks directly to our hearts and also through the four mediums mentioned. He never contradicts Himself. So there is always perfect harmony between His inward impressions and these four voices.

No impression should be acted on as from above which does not clearly meet these tests. God never asks us to act on uncertainties. To do so is a spiritual crime. "He that doubteth is damned if he eat," and this principle prescribes the doing of anything concerning the rightfulness of which there is doubt.

Impressions from above always meet all four of the above tests, and every impression which is doubtful should be rigidly and prayerfully tried by each. If they are scriptural, right, providential, and reasonable, they may be taken as God's voice, and followed as confidently as the angel brought to earth the tidings of our Savior's birth. Otherwise, impressions should be firmly rejected lest they lead into folly, fanaticism, and final ruin.

While the above tests are sufficient and final, the following facts are also worthy of notice in this connection.

Divine impressions are persuasive. God does not drive, but leads His children. Impressions from other sources are loud, clamorous, feverish, and seek to drown the Spirit's voice.

G. D. Watson says, "You can detect the devil by one or two things. The devil always talks loud. Jesus always talks low and tender. I'm talking Greek unless you have ears to hear. 'He that hath ears to hear, let him hear.' When a spirit makes an impression on my mind, that impression can be made in a loud, boisterous, rushing, pell-mell sort of way, or that conviction can come quietly and gently and sweetly. When the devil makes an impression on people's hearts, and when he speaks to the soul, he talks loudly. I mean to say that the impression has a loudness in the mind. I am talking mentally now."

Impressions from above always give sufficient time to the honest seeker to test their genuineness. Those from below are in a hurry, and, fearing detection, clamor for immediate decisions.

"The devil wants you," continues Watson, "to be in a hurry and rush and go pell-mell and not wait for anything; whereas Jesus is always quiet. He is calm and always takes His time. Sometimes, in business matters, the devil makes us think we have got to rush and transact a piece of business without taking time to pray. But when you take things to God in prayer and you wait, if God makes an impression on the mind, it always comes gently, tenderly. You wait on and it will come again, gently, tenderly.

The more you wait on God, if the conviction comes from the Holy Ghost, the more you wait, and the more you pray, the weaker it grows. You can tell by that. If you have a call to some mission work or anything, and you say, 'I wish I did know whether it were God or Satan,' you just take time. If the world is on fire, and your house half burned down, you take time and wait on God."

While it is true, when duty is clearly known, that "the king's business requireth haste," yet when it is not clearly known it is just as true that "he that believeth shall not make haste."

My friend who was recently cheated out of one hundred dollars would have been saved a costly lesson had he waited, prayed, considered, and tested the matter.

Impressions from above welcome the light. Those from below shrink back from it. The first love to be catechized; the second are afraid of tests, and don't like to be questioned. Adam and Eve, when following those from above, were possessed of innocent and holy boldness, and delighted in the divine presence; afterward, they instinctively sought to hide from God's searching eye.

Impressions from above, when followed, are attended by a sweet peace and the consciousness that they are right; those from below, by perplexity and the feeling that something is wrong. The first bring rest. The second kind rob of it.

Impressions from above appeal to our higher spiritual instincts; those from below often to our passions, prejudices, fancies, infatuations, and selfish inclinations.

Those from above make us feel "I ought to do so," and if obeyed there comes a sweet and permanent delight in putting the "ought" in practice. Those from below lack this feature, and any gratification will be temporary. A serpent hides in every rose they bring, and soon is felt its fatal sting.

Impressions from below are destitute of spiritual heat. Satan can counterfeit the light of truth, but not the ardent glow of holy love. Hence, impressions from him bring spiritual chill and discomfort instead of warmth and satisfaction.

Impressions from above ripen into convictions. Those from below never do. They may crystallize into desires, or imaginations, or opinions, but never become convictions. The first make men like the apostles after Pentecost so that they "cannot but speak" and pray and act. The latter will apologize for expressing themselves, and are swept away before the former like leaves before a gale. It is a part of the mission of the Holy Spirit to fill us with such convictions that we will be like the "mountains round about Jerusalem," mighty and immovable. The conditions which must be met in order to rightfully apply these tests will be noticed in a succeeding chapter.

The Holy Spirit is an unerring guide, and he who detects and turns from every wrong impression and fully follows Him will be led into "all truth." It should be the aim of every Christian to overcome inattention and forgetfulness and be thus led.

May we each so "try the Spirits," and "watch and pray," that, like God's people of old, we may see our "pillar of cloud by day and of fire by night," and thus led in a "plain path" be enabled to "stand perfect and complete in all the will of God."

In conclusion, let us again review the rightful tests of all impressions, and ever keep in mind that none should be acted upon which does not bear the divine stamp—
SRPR.

Scriptural. In harmony with God's will as revealed in His Word.

Right. In harmony with God's will as revealed in man's

moral consciousness by the law of God, which is written within his moral nature.

Providential. In harmony with God's will as revealed in His providential dealings.

Reasonable. In harmony with God's will as revealed to man's reasoning powers, illuminated by the Holy Spirit.

All impressions which have not this stamp divine are as valueless as railroad tickets without the stamp of the issuing office. The reason why many people are thwarted in their plans and compelled to get off from trains of action upon which they are attempting to ride, is that they act upon impressions which have not this sacred seal.

When an impression has been tried, and is known to be of God, the whole soul should be thrown into it, and it should be firmly, boldly, and persistently acted upon. The Christian then should set his "face like a flint," and turn neither to the right hand nor the left. His feelings may weep, his imaginations fade, perverted Scripture protest, his infatuations die in despair, his impulses and passions be disappointed, his appetites complain, his prejudices and preconceived notions be abandoned, his friends dismayed, his dreams, signs, and chance happenings all prove false prophets, and "Satan rage, and fiery darts be hurled"; yet he will follow "anywhere and everywhere" that God may lead. "Delivered from every false way," he will test the blessedness of the words of the wise Christian philosopher who said, "Happy is he who is not led by mere sights and sounds; not by strange momentary impressions which may come from the disordered senses, from the world or from the devil, but by that clear light which illuminates the intellect, the conscience, and the heart; which is ever consistent with itself and with God's Word and providences, and which has, in reality, for its author, the Comforter, the Holy Ghost.

"He will also prove the preciousness of the promise which declares: 'The Lord shall guide thee continually, and satisfy thy soul in drought, and make fat thy bones: and thou shalt be like a watered garden, and like a spring of water, whose waters fail not' (Isaiah 58:11)."

Glory be to God that such an experience is possible for every one of His children.

*He will guide you
into all truth.*

Impressions from Above: Divine Guidance Guaranteed

Some people are shy of this subject because others have gone into fanaticism over it. They thus lose great enlightenment which otherwise they might enjoy. Is it sensible to starve to death because some people persist in eating too much? Shall we cease traveling because occasionally an accident occurs? Or freeze to death because some people burn themselves?

Yet it would be wiser to do any of the above than to draw back from being "led by the Spirit," simply because some people have abused their privilege. Our privilege to be divinely led is demonstrated beyond a doubt in the four following ways: by inspired promises, by inspired examples, by inspired experiences, and by inspired aspirations.

Inspired promises. The testimony from this source is overwhelming, and sufficient to make assurance doubly sure even if there were no further evidence.

1. In Psalm 32:8, it is written: "I will instruct thee and teach thee in the way which thou shalt go: I will guide thee with mine eye."

God's eye is here represented as looking out the path for His children, His voice as teaching them, and His finger as pointing to the right path.

2. "The steps of a good man are ordered by the Lord: and He delighteth in his way" (Psalm 37:23). This passage shows God's guidance even in "steps." How blessed to know that He will make known what to do, not only in great things, but in the little "steps" which so often cause perplexity. The man is not as "good" as he ought to be who does not claim this guidance, step by step.

3. What a privilege it is to have a wise, earthly adviser. Yet such may err. Hence counsel at every needed point is provided for us in Jesus. Hence looking unto God with perfect assurance, all, like the Psalmist, may exclaim: "Thou shalt guide me with thy counsel, and afterward receive me to glory."

4. In passing through a dense and unknown wilderness, it is a great advantage to have clear directions for the journey; but how much better to have the faithful guide himself to go ahead, and not only tell the way but lead in it.

This world is a dark thicket. Millions have lost their path and perished in it. Glory be to God that He has given us a guidebook, and best of all the presence of an unerring guide. He says, "I will go before thee, and make the crooked places straight: I will break in pieces the gates of brass, and break in sunder the bars of iron."

By His providences He thus prepares the paths in which He leads His children. Red seas and walled Jerichos are blown out of the way by His almighty breath.

5. "But the Comforter, which is the Holy Ghost, whom the Father will send in my name, he shall teach you all things, and bring all things to your remembrance, whatsoever I have said unto you" (John 14:26). It is the special mission of the Holy Spirit to divinely direct. However, He does not do this independently. The "all things," which it is promised that He shall teach and remind of, are the words of Jesus: "Whatsoever I have said unto you."

He unfolds no new principles, but simply reminds us of and helps us to understand those already revealed. It is just as truly the mission of the Spirit to do this work as it was of the Son to die for us.

6. "Howbeit when he, the Spirit of truth, is come, he will guide you into all truth: for he shall not speak of himself; but whatsoever he shall hear, that shall he speak: ... He shall glorify me: for he shall receive of mine, and shall shew it unto you" (John 16:13, 14).

Here He is represented as a guide. He will lead into "all truth." Jesus declares the "all truth" to be the truth revealed by Him. "He shall receive of mine, and shall shew it unto you"; the truth Jesus proclaims may be likened to a beautiful temple filled with all that the spiritual man needs to meet all the demands of his being for time and for eternity. These things are all unseen to the natural eye. The Spirit prepares the heart, and then leads the soul on and on, higher and higher, through the aisles and labyrinths of this temple, unfolding its secrets, explaining its mysteries, and bringing out its beauties until we are lost "in wonder, love, and praise."

7. "If any of you lack wisdom, let him ask of God, that giveth to all men liberally, and upbraideth not; and it shall be given him" (James 1:5).

Note the following points in this precious promise: guidance for all: "If any of you lack"; guidance from God: "let him ask of God"; guidance given without grudging: "giveth to all men liberally"; guidance positively assured: "it shall be given him."

These, and other kindred promises, make more firm than the mighty mountains the foundation upon which the child of God can base his assurance of being led. They challenge the present appropriating faith of all who are meeting the conditions upon which they are given. They are a priceless parcel of the many "exceeding great and precious promises: that by these ye might be partakers of the divine nature."

Promises of pardon cover all our guilt. Promises of purity, all our pollution. Promises of power, all our weakness. And these promises for being divinely led cover all our perplexity in regard to action. No wonder the poet sings:

> Precious promise God has given,
> To the weary passerby,
> All the way from earth to heaven,
> I will guide thee with mine eye.

The revelation of the Christian's privilege and his wealth in these promises opened up to my own mind a vision of wonderful possibilities which had hitherto been hid. It is just as glorious a privilege to trust these promises for guidance as it is to trust other promises for salvation. Glory be to God for the abundant provision He has made, not only to cover all our sin but to supply all our need.

Inspired examples. Enoch was so divinely led that he continually "walked with God," and followed His counsels so fully that there is no record of his slightest deviation.

Abraham not only received great spiritual blessings, but appropriated God's guidance so completely that he was divinely directed in his travels, in choosing his homestead, in his knowledge of the doom of Sodom, and in accumulating an immense fortune.

The stories of Jacob, of Joseph, of Moses, of a nation led by a pillar of cloud by day and of fire by night, are replete with illustrations of how God's people have looked to and been marvelously led by Him.

All the mistakes, the wanderings, and the captivity of His people came because they failed to hear and heed His voice; but whenever they listened He revealed Himself and granted the needed wisdom. The explicit directions which He unfolded for the construction of the tabernacle, and afterward of the temple, are but illustrations of His ability and willingness to give minute directions at every needed point, no matter how small it may be, to all who are "workers together with Him."

Joshua must have been fully instructed, or he could not have fully followed. Daniel, divinely directed, was meet for every emergency, and his wisdom was a wonder to the world.

Not only were the illustrious lights of Old Testament history thus divinely led, but there were also numberless stars of lesser magnitude whose beams were hid in the obscurity of the humbler walks of life; yet who, guided by God's hand, moved and shone "as the sun when he goeth forth in his might."

They were so firm in their convictions that their actions were prompted by the Unseen One, that rather than do violence to their divine instructions, they submitted to be "stoned," "sawn asunder," and "slain with the sword." Oh, for an army of such heroes. Souls so possessed of the idea that they are actuated in all things by the power that upholds suns and systems, that they will die rather than turn traitor to it.

The New Testament firmament is no less resplendent with stars, whose orbits are divinely made, than is the Old. It opens with Joseph, Mary, Simeon, and the wise men from the East, who will ever beam brightly as examples of those who have tested God's promises to fully guide. The Gospels shine with the dazzling splendor of Him who, in His humanity as our example, ever so fully learned the Father's will that He always said and did those things, and those only that were pleasing in His sight.

The Acts of the Apostles teems with telling incidents illustrating this principle. The apostles were "filled with the Spirit" and "led by the Spirit." They could not have been led by Him had they not first learned His leadings.

The promise which Jesus gave them that He would teach them how to answer their enemies, and that the Spirit of the Father should speak through them, found such fruitful fulfillment that all their adversaries "were not able to resist the wisdom and spirit" by which they spake.

They were gifted with such divine wisdom that they outwitted both ecclesiastical intrigue and Roman power, and while the cry "crucify Him" was still echoing from Mount Calvary, they had established a kingdom which will flourish when Jerusalem and Rome are forgotten—even forever.

Inspired experiences. In addition to the inspired examples recorded in the Word, there are also the experiences of all of God's children who "abide under the shadow of the Almighty," attesting the same truth.

Among the many remarkable instances of guidance recorded in the autobiography of Madame Guyon, who shone amid the darkness of papal superstition like the sun through a thundercloud, we quote the following. It relates to a complex business matter, which, unaided, she could not have handled: "The day when the trial was to come on, after prayer I felt myself strongly pressed to go to the judges. I was wonderfully assisted therein, even so as to discover and unravel all the turns and artifices of this affair, without knowing how I could have been able to do it. . . . God enabled me to manifest the truth in so clear a light, and give me such power to my words that the intendant thanked me for having so seasonably come to undeceive, and set him right in the affair. Had I not done this he assured me the cause had been lost."

Through prayer and faith God thus gave wisdom to this illustrious saint, and it was this wisdom which made her illustrious. She followed the divine voice so fully that she could say: "It seemed to me that my soul became like the New Jerusalem spoken of in the Apocalypse, prepared as a bride for her husband, and where there is no woe, sorrow, or sighing.

"I had a union so great with the good will of God, that my own will seemed entirely lost. My soul could not incline itself on one side or the other, since another will had taken the place of its own, but only nourished itself with the daily providences of God."

Thus led by the Word, the Spirit, and daily providences, she continued to glow with increasing splendor until she passed to her celestial home.

"The Living God," says George Müller, "is my partner." I have not sufficient wisdom to meet these difficulties, so as to be able to know what steps to take, but He is able to direct me. What I have therefore to do is this: in simplicity to spread my case before my heavenly Father and my Lord Jesus. They are my partners. I have to tell out my heart to God, and as I have no wisdom in myself to meet all the many difficulties which continually occur in my business, I ask Him that He would be pleased to guide and direct me, and supply me with the needful wisdom. Then I have to believe that God will do so, and go with good courage to my business, and expect help from Him in the next difficulty that may come before me. I have to look out for guidance; I have to expect counsel from the Lord, and as assuredly as I do so, I shall have it; I shall find that I am not nominally but really in partnership with the Father and with the Son."

By claiming this guidance, Müller was enabled to "remove mountains" of difficulty, and God through him has wrought marvels which will inspire the faith and zeal of His children while the world stands.

Frances Ridley Havergal, whose songs and books have thrilled the Christian world, in all things claimed this blessed privilege. Making mention of it in its application to the use of means she says: "We look up to our Lord for guidance to lay out His money prudently and rightly, and as He would have us lay it out. The gift or garment is selected under His eye, and with conscious reference to Him as our dear Master, for whose sake we shall give it, or in whose service we shall wear it, and whose own silver and gold we shall pay for it, and then it is all right."

Numberless living witnesses join their testimony to the many who have gone before, that God is a true, sure, constant, and wonderful Counselor, and that His guidance is accessible to all who meet the conditions upon which it is promised.

Inspired aspirations. There is a heaven-born aspiration in the heart of every truly converted person to be divinely led. Without such leading there is a deep sense of inability to solve life's problems and meet its perplexities.

All other human needs are met and satisfied in Jesus, and this one is no exception. For guilt there is provided pardon. For pollution, purity. For weakness, power. For spiritual hunger, the Bread of Life. For spiritual thirst, the Water of Life. For spiritual sickness, the Great Physician. For spiritual poverty, an eternal inheritance. For spiritual guidance, divine wisdom.

God creates the desire to receive this wisdom because He has made provision to give it, and the very fact that He inspires it is a token that He has it to give. God does not create desires in men to mock them with fruitless longings, but because He loves to supply their every need, and has planned so to do. This reason, combined with those before mentioned, shows conclusively our privilege in all things to avail ourselves of the services of a mighty counselor. His unerring eye will lead us in the way that we should go. With Him enthroned within, neither poverty nor distance need keep us from His counsels, nor from knowing and doing His will.

In the light of the fourfold testimony given, there remains not a shadow of doubt as to God's ability and willingness to lead all who will follow His instructions. Glorious privilege! The conditions upon which it may be realized are simple, plain, and important, and will be noticed further on.

He leadeth me! O blessed thought,
O words with heav'nly comfort fraught;
Whate'er I do, where'er I be,
Still 'tis God's hand that leadeth me.

He leadeth me! He leadeth me!
By His own hand He leadeth me;
His faithful follower I would be,
For by His hand He leadeth me.

Sometimes 'mid scenes of deepest gloom,
Sometimes where Eden's bowers bloom,
By waters still, o'er troubled sea,
Still 'tis His hand that leadeth me.

Lord, I would clasp Thy hand in mine,
Nor ever murmur nor repine—
Content, whatever lot I see,
Since 'tis my God that leadeth me.

And when my task on earth is done,
When, by Thy grace the victory's won,
E'en death's cold wave I will not flee,
Since God through Jordan leadeth me.

Then keep thy conscience sensitive,
No inward token miss,
And go where grace entices thee,
Perfection lies in this.

Impressions from Above: How to Be Led by Them

In order to be at one's best for detecting impressions from below, and being led by those from above, the following conditions must be met:

Conversion. The unregenerate heart is a camera prepared for impressions from below, and it receives them as greedily as the parched earth drinks in a shower. It has no affinity for those from above, but resolutely repels them. All of its telegraph wires are manipulated by the enemy, and it is with great difficulty that its King can reach it with a message. Of such it is truly said: "For this people's heart is waxed gross, and their ears are dull of hearing, and their eyes they have closed; lest at any time they should see with their eyes, and hear with their ears, and . . . be converted, and I should heal them" (Matthew 13:15). Conversion opens our spiritual eyes and ears, and enables us to discern the spirits whether they be of God.

Purity. Inbred sin in the heart of the believer is a great hindrance to being divinely led. It is like dust in the eye which pains and blinds it; like wax in the ear which deadens the hearing.

Watson writes that the most formidable foe of the devil on earth is the sanctified believer: "After you are sanctified

75

the devil comes up to you and hunts all around and says, 'Where is my instrument gone? I could run my fingers over the carnal mind and play a tune in this man's soul.' He finds no wire in your soul to pull on now. He used to pull on your judgment and reason and carnal nature, but that is all gone and he finds nothing but Christ.

"When the devil finds out he has no territory in you, he gets mad, flings off his coat, and begins to blaspheme. He will say, 'You have professed holiness, and you know you haven't it.' You never know how plainly the devil can talk to you until you are sanctified. Before he could run into the back door of your heart and pull the wires; but after you are sanctified the devil has got to fight you on the outside. He will come to your face and tell you you are not sanctified, and you know it! He will threaten you with falling; he will talk to you intellectually, and pronounce words in your mind.

"Before we are sanctified the method of the devil is to work in Christian people through their carnal mind without letting them know it is the devil. He will come to Christian men, to Christian women, ministers, good people who are endeavoring to serve God and are on the way to heaven; he will work his plans and purposes upon them by using their carnal mind, and so work that they think it is their wisdom. The devil will come to an unsanctified Christian who is converted, and will put a certain idea into his mind or heart, and he will say, 'Now, isn't that wise, isn't that prudent, isn't that cautious?' Thus he will work on their prudential motives, on their reason, and on their carnal fears. He will work on their man-fearing spirit; he will work on their worldly policy and their worldly wisdom, making a playground upon their carnal mind.

"Now, mark you, he has no possession of God's children, but he will annoy them and disturb them and hinder them. They are doing ten thousand things in which they do not dream they are doing the devil's work. The devil goes to Christian people and gets them to have a church theatrical. He wouldn't dare have them start a regular theater with all the accessories, but he goes and works on their worldly policy and their worldly mind, so that when they have got these things up, church members do not know they are doing the devil's work. They say, 'We are doing this to raise money for our church. It is laudable.' They think they are doing right. They simply are doing the devil's work by the devil's suggestions, only the devil is hiding himself, and laughing at them all the while."

If, then, we would be at our best to detect the impressions which are continually coming to us, we, having our hearts "purified by faith," must be cleansed from inbred sin.

George Müller urges the Christian to "only maintain an upright heart. But if you live in sin, if you willfully and habitually do things which you know to be contrary to the will of God, then you can not expect to be heard by Him. 'If I regard iniquity in my heart the Lord will not hear me.' "

There must be a belief that God will make His guidance known. "If any of you lack wisdom, let him ask of God, who giveth to all men liberally, and upbraideth not; and it shall be given him. But let him ask in faith, nothing wavering. For he that wavereth is like a wave of the sea driven with the wind and tossed. For let not that man think he shall receive any thing of the Lord" (James 1:5-7).

Unbelief in God's ability and promises to guide will leave the soul like a ship at sea with no helm and at the mercy of wind and waves.

There must be complete commitment to God. Hence it is written, "Commit thy way unto the Lord; trust also in him; and he shall bring it to pass." Any mental reservation in the commitment will deaden the discerning of the divine voice.

Spurgeon said, "Brethren, I can testify for my God that when I have submitted my will to His directing Spirit, I have always had reason to thank Him for His wise counsel. But when I have asked at His hands, having already made up my own mind, I have had my own way; but like as He fed the Israelites with quails from heaven, while the meat was yet in their mouth, the wrath of God came upon them."

He who employs a physician or attorney puts the case fully in their hands and follows their directions. Jesus is the soul's Great Physician, and the lost man's lawyer. Infinite in wisdom and in love, the most timid soul need not fear to commit itself unreservedly to Him. Any shrinking here may cost what is worth more than worlds. The soul must be like a ship sailing under sealed orders unrevokably committed to execute the orders when opened, no matter what they are. It is God's to direct; ours to execute. We are accountable only for the execution; He for the results. Praise His name!

Unless it is a settled question with us that we will follow God's guidance when it is clearly revealed, at any cost, we can never know it, but will be a prey of impressions from below.

I heard a minister say that there had been times when he would pray for light on certain subjects, and then get up and hurry away lest he would get an answer that he would not like. Such seekers arise from their knees but to stumble on in darkness. We must not only "commit our ways" unto God, but also the time and manner of them.

"God," says an eminent minister, "not only requires us to obey and serve Him, but to obey and serve Him in His own time and way. In the eye of God voluntary disobedience in the manner of a thing is the same as disobedience in the thing itself."

He who consents to obey God, but seeks to dictate the

time of so doing, is as unwise as a blacksmith that would hammer the iron either before it is heated or after it cools off instead of when it is hot and flexible. Had Joshua dictated as to the time and manner of taking Jericho, Israel doubtless would have been defeated, and his own name have sunk into oblivion. For transgression in the manner of obedience, Moses was debarred from the promised land.

God said to David, "When thou hearest the sound of a going in the tops of the mulberry trees, . . . then thou shalt bestir thyself: for then shall the Lord go out before thee, to smite the . . . Philistines."

There is a mighty significance in the two "thens" in the preceding paragraph. "*Then* thou shalt bestir thyself, for *then* shall the Lord go out before thee."

Confusion ever comes to all who say "now" when God says "tomorrow," and who say "tomorrow" when God says "now."

Acknowledgment. Another divinely decreed condition of guidance is acknowledgment. "In all thy ways acknowledge him, and he shall direct thy paths" (Proverbs 3:6). As justification is conditioned on an acknowledgment of Jesus as a personal Savior, and entire sanctification, an acknowledgment of the Holy Ghost as a personal sanctifier, so divine guidance is conditioned on the acknowledgment of the Spirit as a personal guide. Nor will a wholesale theoretical acknowledgment answer this purpose.

"In all thy ways" implies claiming His counsels in things small as well as great. We have scriptural warrant for acknowledging God in everything that is of as much concern to us as one of the hairs of our heads.

To withhold this hearty specific acknowledgment is as if a patient should decline to counsel with his physician on minor matters relating to disease, and refuse to own the complete committal of his case into his physician's hands. God will not honor those who would avail themselves of the advantages of His counsels, but are ashamed to own that they are thus divinely directed. "In all thy ways" means business "ways," home "ways," church "ways," private "ways," public "ways," all "ways." May we each meet this condition, and test the blessedness of the promise, and whether we need wisdom to find a "lost key" or to prepare a revival sermon, verily, it will be given.

Goodness. "The steps of a good man are ordered by the Lord: and he delighteth in his way" (Psalm 37:23). The bad follow their own counsels and suffer the consequences, but the "good" man meets all the conditions whereby he is enabled to distinguish between impressions from below and voices from above, and hence his very "steps," as well as the path of his life, are ordered by God. No "step" should be taken which is not thus ordered. In the light of this bright and blessed promise there need not be. This is one of the special favors which God lavishes upon the "good."

Patience. "Rest in the Lord, and wait patiently for him" (Psalm 37:7). Jesus never seemed hurried, and yet how busy! He who tramples beneath his feet the great scriptural truth that "he that believeth shall not make haste," and is too hurried to candidly canvass the matter, and closes his eyes to reason and God's providences, is "too much possessed of self or satanic influences" to be led by holy influences. In order to be divinely led we must, says Upham, "cease from self and from its turbulent and deceitful elements; cease to place ourselves and our personal interests foremost and keep our own plans, purposes, and aims in entire subjection. For instance, when we ask God to guide us, we must not at the same time cherish in our hearts a secret determination and hope to guide ourselves. . . . The existence of undue eagerness of spirit is an evidence that we are in some degree afraid to trust God, and that we are still too much under the life of nature."

God says, "Be still, and know that I am God," and such stillness is frequently necessary to enable one to discern the harmony of the four voices through which God speaks to the soul.

All who can say with the Psalmist, "I waited patiently for the Lord," will soon with him be able to add, "and he inclined unto me, and heard my cry."

He who attempts to test impressions in a nervous and hurried way, is as unwise as he who would listen to a response from a telephone in that manner. In both cases confusion instead of satisfaction will be the result.

Humility. The proud, self-willed man seeks not to know God's voice. Vocies from below with him drown out all others. Not the haughty but "the meek will he guide in judgment: and the meek will he teach his way." From the wise and prudent and self-sufficient, God's guidance is hid, but "revealed unto babes," the teachable, humble, Christlike.

Dependence on God. It is fatal to divine guidance to trust unduly in self, or friends, or books. "Trust in the Lord with all thine heart; and lean not unto thine own understanding" (Proverbs 3:5).

Human understanding is finite and errs. God's is infinite and can not err. Hence the "whole heart" of him who would be divinely led must go out to God for the knowledge of His perfect will.

Guidance must be claimed. Jesus says of this as of all His priceless gifts: "Ask, and ye shall receive."

It must be sought with pure motives. Of those who seek for selfish ends it is written: "Ye ask, and receive not, because ye ask amiss."

Be prepared for surprises. God very probably will not decide as you expect.

"You must remember," writes Hannah W. Smith, "that

our God has all knowledge and all wisdom, and that, therefore, it is very possible He may guide you into paths where He knows great blessings are awaiting you, but which to the shortsighted human eyes around you seem sure to result in confusion and loss. You must recognize the fact that God's thoughts are not as man's thoughts, nor his ways as man's ways; and that He who knows the end of things from the beginning, alone can judge of what the results of any course of action may be."

When Saul of Tarsus cried out, "Lord, what wilt thou have me to do?" the answer was doubtless as surprising to him as a stroke of lightning from a clear sky; but he was ready for the surprise and welcomed it.

When I asked God to reveal His will to me concerning my lifework, I had no more idea of many things that have since been revealed than a heathen has of holiness or heaven.

One must be dead. We must be dead to sin, to self, and dead to the world.

So dead that no desire shall rise
To pass for good, or great, or wise,
In any but my Savior's eyes.

We must be so dead to all voices from sinful and doubtful sources that they will influence our actions no more than if they had been silent. In the stillness of the funeral of self, the voices from the skies are clearly heard. Therefore, "likewise reckon yourselves to be dead indeed unto sin, but alive unto God through Jesus Christ our Lord."

Over such, all impressions from below are received as coldly as caresses by a corpse.

Be filled with the Spirit. This is the all-important preparation. It includes all of the others. It gives an insight into Satan's devices that can be possessed in no other way. It gives the ears a keen discernment that will detect the slightest deviation of any impression from the fourfold harmony.

"To him who is crucified to self," says Watson, "the Holy Spirit grants an illumination and direction, incomprehensible to imperfect believers. He can discern in the providence of the Father a special significance and minuteness to which others are blind. He can detect clear indications of God's will in the written Word over which others grossly stumble, and besides these he can hear that inner voice of the Spirit, can know the touches of a divine finger on his soul impelling him along his God-given orbit."

Fully possessed of the Spirit, the soul becomes a magnet which draws to itself all good impressions, but leaves the dross behind. It is, therefore, a qualification of being divinely led of such paramount importance that Jesus would allow no preacher, after the opening of the Holy Ghost dispensation, to go forth without it, and the church in its purity, fresh from the mind of God, selected only those thus filled to oversee her temporal concerns (see Acts 6:3).

He who meets the above conditions will be at his best to discern the nature of all impressions. Though like Job he may sometimes be sorely tried, yet God will not permit him to "walk in darkness."

Above all the din of voices which are not divine, he will be able to hear the still, small voice saying: "This is the way, walk ye in it." Though Satan may come as an "angel of light," yet his presence will pale before the celestial sunshine which illuminates within, and his icy waves of false light will be lost amid the burning beams of the sun which never sets. Hallelujah!

If ye know these things,
happy are ye
if ye do them.

JOHN 13:17

EIGHT

Practical Applications

Let us apply the preceding principles to a few practical matters such as are constantly coming up for decision.

A call to the ministry. A young man finds himself the subject of a strong impression to devote his life to the ministry. He is an honest believer and anxious to make no mistake. He knows that such an impression may come from Satan, friends, or fancy, and desires not to be deceived on the one hand, nor to resist God on the other.

He commits all to God, asks for promised wisdom from above, and then proceeds to see if the leading bears the divine stamp: **SRPR.**

1. **S.** Is it scriptural? It is evident that a call to the ministry is in harmony with the Word. So he does not need to tarry long at this point.

2. **R.** Is it right for him to respond to such a call? If he finds that in so doing his circumstances are such that he will be compelled to wrong his family, or his creditors, or others, that fact will settle the matter, either that the impression is not of God, or else that the time has not come to put it in practice. If, however, all is right, he is prepared to pass to the next test.

3. **P.** If the impression is of God the way will open for him either to begin the work or to prepare for it.

85

When God calls a person to preach he notifies the church of the fact, and she, if awake, opens the door for him. Sometimes, however, she is asleep, and hence does not hear this summons from her Head.

I know of a young man whom God called to preach. The Word was "like fire shut up in his bones." His gifts were not as apparent on the surface as with some, and pastor and official board, after considering his case, declined granting even an exhorter's license. He kept right with God and awaited providential indications. At once doors opened, and invitations came for him to aid in revival meetings. He did so. Great success attended his labors. Scores and hundreds were converted. The pastor and official board saw their mistake, and unsolicited, reconsidered his case, sent him a local preacher's license, and he became one of the most successful soul-winning pastors in the Michigan Conference.

The way always opens if the call is of God, for of all such it is written: "Behold, I have set before thee an open door, and no man can shut it."

4. **R**. Next comes the application of the final test—is it reasonable? A person unenlightened by the Holy Ghost, and trained to think that success lies only in the accumulation of cash, would say no.

But God's child, with divinely anointed eyes, will see things differently. If he has no voice or other gifts for the work, either hidden or manifest, that will settle the matter; but if he has, and the above tests are all met, then this one will soon be settled. Given the fact that over 800 million souls have never heard the Gospel, the fact that the demand for a wise, consecrated Spirit-baptized ministry is always greater than the supply, that an avalanche of souls is rushing to doom each year with no effort being made to save them, and common sense responds in the affirmative—"Yes, it is reasonable"—and these four voices through which God speaks to men's minds unite with the Spirit's call, and the conviction that he must preach becomes so strong that, like Paul, he feels, "Woe is unto me, if I preach not the Gospel." If the "fulness of the Spirit" be claimed, the ministry will soon become the delight of his life.

I well remember my own experience at this point. I had always felt that if I was converted I would be called to preach. Soon after my conversion, the words, "Go ye into all the world and preach the Gospel," were applied to me in a wonderful way. I felt that God was calling me. I was "unspeakably" different, and did not see how I could ever succeed, but dared not say so. I mentioned it to but one person, but did all I could to prepare for it. I was assured that it was scriptural and right, but the way did not open to preach for over four years. I began my studies preparatory to conference examination, and felt sure in my heart that God would unfold the gift within in some way, and that in His time the way would open.

It opened first by my being given charge of a rural Sunday school, and next by being called to preach in a neglected neighborhood, where a revival at once broke out. When conference came I was duly recommended and given work, and God has let the fire fall all along. To Him be glory forever!

To a woman called to preach, the way of work often seems more hedged up than to a man, because the church may not officially recognize her call, or provide for her preparation to fill it as with her brother. God, however, if He be fully followed, will open a way through every hedge, and lead His loyal children to the work to which He calls; and the fourfold test being met, they will be as certain of the divinity of their call as of their own existence.

I know a successful woman preacher, wife of a Methodist minister, who, when called to preach, was firmly opposed by her father. All the tests of a genuine call were met, but his opposition continued to increase. She was of age, but shrank from crossing her father's will. Finally a call came to aid in revival work. She felt that she must obey God rather than man, and decided to accept it. "Tell Bro. ——— that you come without your father's consent," was the painful message which followed her from her father's lips as she left her home for the ripe harvest field. She had scarcely reached her destination, however, when a letter reached her from him giving full and free consent.

God tested her obedience and tried her faith, and then melted the opposition, and blessed her ministry to the salvation of many. In His own time and manner He will thus level all mountains which are in the way of all who fully follow Him.

A call to mission work can be tested the same as a call to the ministry.

Marriage. Usefulness and happiness for life may depend upon the rightful settlement of this question. How can people be sure their union is of God? Shall fancy, feeling, or infatuation decide the matter, or shall it be submitted to reason, right, and God? Let us apply the tests. Two persons are drawn toward each other, and feel that perhaps they should be one.

1. **S.** First of all they ask, "Would our union be scriptural?" They find on general principles that marriage is commended in the Word. God instituted it. He declares that "it is not good that the man should be alone," and that "marriage is honourable in all."

They apply the principles of Scripture to their own peculiar cases. If one proves to be an unconverted person, then the explicit Scripture command, "Be ye not unequally yoked together with unbelievers," makes further testing needless. Many rush blindly over this mandate to regret it when it is too late.

It may be that both are believers, but that one of them is divorced from a former companion for other than the one cause for which Scripture allows divorce, and that, therefore, it would be an adulterous union.

A member of a church of which I was pastor, once called for me to perform his marriage ceremony. He was a noble Christian man. I asked him a few questions, and soon learned that his proposed wife had a husband living, and while divorced by the law of the land, he was not sure that the sin on the part of her husband set her free by the law of Christ. I read to him Matthew 5:32, and parallel passages, and explained to him that on account of these Bible truths I was not free to perform the ceremony.

"Then," said he, "I am not free to have it performed." He continued, "She is the only woman I ever loved, but I should have thought of this before. I dread to break the news to her, but I must be true to Christ." He was all broken down, but remained loyal to his convictions.

2. **R.** The sanction of Scripture being secured, then comes the test: Is it right? Will it wrong anyone? Is there any physical or other disability?

At this point the Christian will remember that it is written: "Whatsoever ye do in word or deed, do all in the name of the Lord Jesus," and also further that, "whatsoever ye do, do all to the glory of God."

If he finds that he is actuated by some minor motive, like the gratification of self, or bettering his position in society, or gaining wealth, or merely getting a housekeeper, and that God's glory is not his chief aim in the matter, he should wait until he knows that it is.

3. **P.** Next, does the way open? Providential barriers at this point have often settled this as well as other questions. If uncontrollable circumstances make the union an impossibility, that proves the divine seal is not upon it, or that it must be deferred.

4. **R**. Finally, is it reasonable? Tastes may be so different, education so diverse, ambitions so opposed, and temperaments so unfitting, that this alone would show that they are not divinely mated.

But where these tests are all met, and there exists on the part of both persons a conviction that God unites them, and this conviction deepens as the days fly, there can be no doubt as to its divinity.

The careful application of these principles would prevent many hasty, unwise, and unscriptural marriages, and hence dry up the fountain which feeds so many divorces.

It would lead to such unions as God delights to own, families whose days would be as the "days of heaven upon earth."

The baptism of the Holy Spirit. Every believer soon after conversion feels a heart longing for the blessed baptism of the Holy Spirit, which will fully cleanse from all inbred sin, and thus give complete victory over fear, impatience, unbelief, pride, and all the uprisings which are felt from time to time in the heart which has not accepted the Holy Spirit as its complete sanctifier. This longing may find but incomplete expression, yet a deep heart hunger is there, and craves satisfaction.

A strong impression soon comes to such a soul that complete victory is provided through the atonement, that God requires entire holiness, and that it should be sought and received as definitely as conversion. Flying to the fourfold tests for light, it is found first.

1. **S**. The feeling is scriptural. God commands, "Be ye holy." The Word also declares, "Be filled with the Spirit"; "This is the will of God, even your sanctification"; and, "For God hath not called us unto uncleanness, but unto holiness."

It also promises cleansing from "all filthiness of the

flesh and spirit," and that "we being delivered out of the hand of our enemies might serve him without fear, in holiness and righteousness before him, all the days of our life."

Jesus also promised that He would send the Holy Spirit, and commanded His disciples to tarry until they received Him. The apostles and members of the early church received this gift, and the Word declares that it is for all believers.

Prophets, apostles, and Jesus possessed this experience, and under its influence their lives glowed with holy fire.

Scripture command, precept, promise, experience, and prophecy all combine to show that every believer may claim by faith this precious legacy, and be as conscious that the Holy Spirit fully sanctifies as he is that Jesus fully forgives. Glory be to God for such assurance!

2. **R**. In regard to the rightfulness of such an experience there can be no doubt. If it is right to obey God, to be pure, and live a holy life, then this is right.

3. **P**. Next, is it attainable? If the conditions of receiving it are such that they cannot be met, then all are providentially debarred from this privilege. On the other hand, however, they are simple, plain, and practicable. A complete consecration which yields every power and possession entirely to God forever, and then a present faith in the promises which offer the gift of the Holy Ghost, are the sole conditions upon which this priceless boon is granted. These conditions all can meet who will, so that this voice unites with the two preceding, in proclaiming that the impulse to be filled with the Spirit is of God.

4. **R**. That such an experience is "a reasonable service," is seen from the following facts: God commands it and promises it; the wisest and most successful saints have claimed it and proclaimed it; it satisfies the longings of the

91

soul; it delivers from setbacks, and gives new power to work for God and resist the devil; it convinces the world as nothing else will of the divinity of our religion; God has given it to all who have met the conditions, and "He is no respector of persons"; it is the only thing that will enable one to be perfectly holy; without it it is impossible to be free from carnality; with it growth in grace is greatly facilitated; without it, our joy cannot be full; it casts out all slavish fear; and it pleases God and makes its possessor like Jesus.

For these, and many other reasons, it is seen beyond a doubt that this leading bears the closest scrutiny of reason, who joins her overwhelmingly convincing testimony with that of the three other judges declaring the divinity of this impulse—an impulse which with multitudes has become such a conviction as to lead them out into the boundless ocean of Jesus' perfect love.

Associates. There are so many societies and lodges which crowd their claims upon people that the question of affiliation with them often arises. Such action should be summoned before these scrutinizing tests.

1. **S.** If the society has only worldly aims, is controlled by worldly people, and is sustained by worldly expedients, then the Scripture commands, "Come out from among them, and be ye separate," and, "be not conformed to this world," should settle the matter without further investigation.

2. **R.** Would affiliation with it be right? Would time and money thus spent be for the glory of God? Would it lead to saying or doing anything of which Jesus would not approve?

3. **P.** Is the way open for spending the time which would be thus taken without infringing on other sacred duties? Is there no other providential barrier?

4. **R.** Is it reasonable to unite with it? Will spirituality

be blurred or brightened? Is it the best investment for the time and money it will take?

Will my example in uniting be such as I will be glad to have young converts and others follow? Have I reason to believe that Jesus would do likewise were He in my place? If there is doubt about a rightful answer to any of the above questions, reason will demand a stop, and refuse to affix her signet until the doubt disappears. He who turns a deaf ear to any one of these four friendly counselors does so at his peril, and sooner or later will find that he has grasped thorns instead of roses.

Tobacco. Apply these principles to the use of tobacco, a habit which counts its slaves by the million, and we find that duty in the matter is clearly declared.

1. **S**. Scripture commands, "Be ye clean, that bear the vessels of the Lord," and, "whatsoever ye do, do all to the glory of God." As its use is a manifest violation of each of these principles, it must ever lack the sacred seal of Holy Writ.

2. **R**. Right affirms that its use is wrong, because it pollutes the breath, impairs the health, fosters disease, sets a bad example, wastes money, and transgresses both the principles and precepts of the Bible.

3. **P**. Providence points to the many ways that the money thus worse than wasted could be wisely used.

4. **R**. Reason shouts "amen" to the decisions of her three sister voices, and emphasizes the folly of chewing up and squirting out or smoking away money that might be used to glorify God.

In his excellent book on the offices of the Holy Spirit, Clark says that, in many cases, God's will has already been revealed:

"Whenever the will of God is clearly revealed in the Bible in regard to any subject, our duty in regard to that subject is determined. We are not to expect an inward revelation in addition to the outward one to show us what to do.

"If Jesus says, 'Do not kill, do not steal, do not bear false witness, defraud not, honor thy father and mother,' we need no other revelation in regard to our duty in these particulars.

"And the Scriptures do go into more detailed directions than we should imagine, until we acquaint ourselves thoroughly with them. If the Christian lady wishes to know how she may dress so as to please God, she finds that women are 'to adorn themselves in modest apparel'; and with God's providence and the Holy Spirit to assist the sincere inquirer in determining, I think few would be left longer in doubt.

"If we want to know what kind of talk is acceptable to God, we read (1) that we are to let no corrupt communication proceed out of our mouth, nor any foolish talking, and (2) that our talk ought to be good 'to the use of edifying.'

"If we are in doubt how to treat our enemies and those who have injured us, we are told explicitly, 'Love your enemies,' 'Pray for them that despitefully use you,' and 'Avenge not yourselves.' And if our civil or personal rights are invaded, we are asked, 'Why do ye not rather suffer wrong than go to law?' and told that charity, which is perfect love, 'seeketh not her own.' And the universal duty of Christians when praying is, 'Forgive, if ye have aught against any man.'

"If we want to understand our obligations to the civil magistrates and rules, we are told to honor them, to obey them in all things, not in conflict with our duty to the King of kings, to pray for them, and to pay tribute to them.

"If we are at a loss as to how far we may join in the pleasures and customs of the world, we are enjoined not to be conformed to the world, and assured that 'if any man love the world, the love of the Father is not in him.' It is to the written Word then that we are first to look for the knowledge of our Christian duties as well as for the knowledge of salvation."

In applying these tests, all light should be welcomed, the Scriptures should be diligently studied, good books read, wise counselors conferred with. Above all, the presence and guidance of the Holy Spirit should be constantly claimed.

All the conditions mentioned in the preceding chapter should also be met. Converted, cleansed, filled, acknowledging God's guidance, persistently praying and believing for it, and patiently waiting for and expecting it in the use of all known means, it will be freely and graciously given.

Only a few of the practical questions which are daily arising have been noticed, but the same process of testing will apply to all. It is the gracious privilege of every Christian in this way to be so assuringly convinced of the truthfulness and divinity of his convictions, that with Isaiah he can exclaim, "For the Lord God will help me; therefore shall I not be confounded: therefore have I set my face like a flint, and I know that I shall not be ashamed."

This book of the law
shall not depart out of thy mouth;
but thou shalt meditate therein
day and night,
that thou mayest observe to do
according to all that is written
therein: for then thou shalt make
thy way prosperous, and then
thou shalt have good success.

JOSHUA 1:8

NINE

Convictions from Above: Results of Being Led by Them

Impressions which are of God ripen into convictions. They are to convictions what the blossom is to the fruit. No impression should be followed until it has thus ripened. When it has, it must be obeyed, and God will always bless such obedience with blessed and abundant fruitage. The results are so sweet and soul-satisfying that simply a review of them is an inspiration.

The following are among the many fruits which abound in all who are thus led:

Calmness. A holy calm possesses the soul which is conscious that God is leading. It may be led contrary to natural inclinations, and like Paul, against the protests of countrymen and bosom friends; yet amid all oppositions, it may be as peaceful as Galilee beneath the Master's silencing command.

Confidence. Righteousness always inspires confidence. The promise that "the Lord shall be thy confidence, and shall keep thy foot from being taken," finds in them fruitful fulfillment. Trusting not in self or human help, but in the "living God" alone, they are as "bold as a lion." They can speak to frowning Sanhedrins, or, like Luther, to an angry Diet, if God gives the message, and fearlessly leave the results with Him. They sow the seed that He commands, and expect Him to send the sunshine, the shower, and the harvest.

They are free from fret. God never leads people to fret and worry. Hence, those who keep all their ways committed to Him, never do. "Anxious for nothing, but in everything with prayer and thanksgiving," they let their requests be known to God, and thus possess the peace that passeth understanding. If the seed they have sown does not come up the next morning, they do not dig it up to see what is the matter, but having done their best, believe that God will do the rest. Instead of fretting and groaning under corroding care, they "cast all their burdens upon the Lord." He sustains them, and they sing:

This is my story, this is my song
Praising my Savior all the day long.

Blessed salvation that saves from sin, and also from friction and from fret!

Humility. All who are divinely led prove the truth that "before honor is humility." They illustrate the truth of Bishop Taylor's statement, that "humility is like a tree whose root when it is set deepest in the earth rises higher and spreads fairer, and stands surer and lasts longer, and every step of its descent is like a rib of iron." The fact that they have no wisdom in themselves, but have to depend upon another at every turn, tends in itself to keep them lowly. Thus, humbling themselves under the mighty hand of God, He exalts them by guiding them with His counsels, and afterward receives them into glory.

The possibility that, through a defective judgment or

some other infirmity, they may be mistaken also makes them very teachable in regard to all points where God's will has not been unmistakably revealed to them. Jesus, our Great Exampler, always divinely led, manifested His humility by divesting Himself of the glory He had with the Father, by taking our nature, by His seemingly humble and ignoble birth, by subjection to His parents, by His occupation as a carpenter, by partaking of our infirmities, by becoming a servant, by associating with the so-called "riff-raff" of society, by refusing earthly honors, by exposing Himself to reproach and contempt, and by His death as an outcast criminal upon the despised cross. All who are fully led by God have in them this mind which was also in Christ Jesus, and "walking as He walked," they live amid the profusion and fragrance of the flowers which bloom only in the vale of humility.

They please God. Like Enoch, they walk with God, and have the testimony that they please Him, because they "keep his commandments, and do those things that are pleasing in his sight." Even when they make mistakes, which through infirmity they are liable to, He does not frown upon them, because He knows they did not mean to, and judges the action by the intention. They prize His smile of approbation more than the plaudits of a universe without it, and this they have. They feel:

Let the world despise and leave me,
They have left my Savior, too,
Human hearts and looks deceive me,
Thou art not like man, untrue;
And while Thou shalt smile upon me,
God of wisdom, love and might,
Foes may hate and friends may shun me,
Show Thy face and all is bright.

Sometimes the Father calls His children to a course which brings censure from worldlings and chiding from friends, and then soothes the pain thus caused by loving caresses which He ravishes upon them when they are all alone with Him. A millionfold repaid for their sacrifices, they exclaim:

Blest Savior, what delightful fare!
How sweet Thine entertainments are!

They are inflexible, and walk by faith. In nonessentials they are as yielding as air, but in matters where God's will is clearly known they are as firm as granite. They belong to the class of whom is said, "These are the men of whom martyrs are made. When the day of great tribulation comes, when dungeons are ready and fires are burning, then God permits His children, who are weak in the flesh, to stand aside; then the illuminated Christians, those who live in the region of high emotion rather than of quiet faith, who have been conspicuous in the world of Christian activity, and have been as a pleasant and loud song, and in many things have nobly done, will unfold to the right and to the left, and let this little company of whom the world is ignorant and whom it cannot know, come up from their secret places to the great battle of the Lord. To them the prison is as acceptable as the throne; a place of degradation as a place of honor. Ask them how they feel and they will perhaps be startled, because their thoughts are thus turned from God to themselves, and they will answer by saying 'what God wills.' They have no feeling separate from the will of God. . . . Hence, chains and dungeons have no terrors; a bed of fire is as a bed of down."

They are reasonable. As the Spirit of God leads men through their reasoning power, those thus led are always ready to give a reason for every position they take and every act they do. The life and work of George Müller, of Bristol Orphanage fame, is a remarkable illustration of this principle. His *Life of Trust* is one of the most exhilarating faith tonics of which we know. He states first that he was led to found his work on scriptural principles. Then he mentions six solid reasons why he took the course he did.

Watson, in his unique sermon on "The Two Veils," says, "Dr. Daniel Steele, one of the most polished men in the world, prayed for sanctification for three weeks, and the thought kept coming up: 'Now, if God sanctifies you, He'll make you act oddly,' and he was afraid he might have to shout in the streetcars, or do some other singular thing. At length the Spirit said to him: 'Don't you think that God has as good sense of what is right as you have? Don't you think that God knows as much about good behavior as you do? Do you think God will do anything foolish?' He saw that it was only a temptation, let loose of everything, and God baptized him with the Holy Ghost so wonderfully that he could hardly eat or sleep for several days. And let me tell you, he has been one of the best behaved men you ever saw since that time, and has not done anything at all foolish."

They meet with opposition. The Holy Spirit often leads contrary to carnal inclinations and the opinions and protests of friends and relatives, and always counter to the world and the devil. Hence, opposition is inevitable. He takes up and carries on the work of Jesus, which is "to destroy the works of the devil," and they, of course, resist Him. Hence, all who fancy that they can be led by the Spirit and please everyone, are doomed to disappointment. As well might an army expect to do its duty, and at the same time please the enemy.

Depravity and the devil no more agree with the leading of the Holy Ghost than fire can mix with water.

They are victorious. God is their leader. He always gives the victory to all who fully follow Him.

From victory unto victory,
His armies shall He lead,
Till every foe is vanquished,
And Christ is Lord indeed.

They rule their own spirits. Appetites and passions bow beneath the mandates of their Divine Master, and led of God they feel that they "can do all things through Christ which strengtheneth." They love to follow their leader, and expect soon to see the day when all enemies shall be put beneath His feet; earth, the old battlefield, burnt up and replaced by another wherein dwelleth righteousness and their King "crowned Lord of all."

They are courteous. As the Holy Spirit leads none to be selfish, all who follow Him will be saved from selfish acts, and thus from all the discourteous ways which selfishness prompts.

A true Christian is in the best sense of that word a true gentleman. Rudeness, coarseness, and selfishness being eliminated; gentleness, refinement, and love are crowned in their stead, and though the outer garb may be coarse and language lame, yet the good breeding of heavenly parentage will appear in all who follow closely their unseen guide.

They readily adjust themselves to God's providential dealings. People who are not thus led, like Saul of Tarsus before his conversion, are ever "kicking against the pricks" of opposing providences. Those who are walking in the light of the interpretations which the Spirit gives them, hear God's voice in all His providential dealings with them. Hence, when fortune fades, or health fails, or friends betray, or enemies slander, or plans perish, or loved ones die, though pained, yet in perfect peace they can say:

Yet still I whisper, "as God will."
And in His hottest fire hold still.

Even when God by His providences performs some painful amputation, they can say, "He doeth all things well," for they know that He is leading, that the pain is needful for their discipline, and that "all things" are being made to work together for their good. When called to suffer, they have learned:

1. To hold still in the furnace. That uneasiness hinders the process and mars the work.

2. Not to question the Refiner too much. He understands His business.

3. That the purgation, though painful, is worth infinitely more than it costs.

4. To accept God's discipline without continually making suggestions to Him.

When storms of opposition break over them, and waves of adversity threaten to engulf, they sing:

My bark is wafted from the strand
By breath divine,
Upon the helm there rests a hand
Other than mine.
He holds me when the tempests shock,
I shall not fall.
If sharp, 'tis short; if long, 'tis light,
He orders all.

The Spirit of God will never lead people to do what the providences of God make it impossible for them to do. I have known people who were strong in their expressions that it was God's will that they should do certain things, when He was continually and emphatically saying no to them by His providences.

"If any impressions or convictions," writes Upham, "which thus involve a contradiction of the voice of the Spirit and the voice of Providence should rest upon the mind of any person, he may be assured that they came from the wrong source, and ought to be rejected. We assert, therefore, that he who is led by the Holy Spirit will find his conduct beautifully harmonizing with the events of divine providence as they daily and hourly develop themselves. Thus people divinely led are saved from the folly of thinking an impression is from above when the way will not open for them to put it in practice.

Duty becomes a pleasure. Though the feelings may at first shrink back from some of the leadings of the Holy Spirit, yet if compelled to yield, like conquered children, they will soon dry their tears and be inexpressibly glad under the right decisions of the will. Who has not wept for grief at some summons from above, and then a little later been thrilled with joy over the same guidance. For of such God says, "I will turn their mourning into joy, and will comfort them, and make them rejoice in their sorrow." Men weep when God takes away their pennies, but rejoice when they see that He only did this that He might replace them with rubies.

There will be seasons of severe temptation. Satan will not allow God's life plan for His children to be executed without doing all in his power to thwart it. To accomplish this purpose he will come in thousands of artful and seemingly innocent ways, as well as by open and direct assault. So the Christian's only safety is to "watch and pray," lest temptation be fallen into.

The Bible will be revered and its teachings obeyed. The Holy Spirit is the author of the Bible, and a part of His work is to explain and apply its teachings. Hence, He never leads to a course which it condemns, but always in harmony with its instructions. Therefore, all who are fully led by Him will shape their acts according to the teachings of the Word; and their lives, like that of Jesus, will be a fulfillment of the principles of Holy Writ. They realize that all impressions which clash with the Word are wrong, and steadfastly resist them.

God cares for the consequences. When God's leadings are rightly followed He takes all the responsibility of the results. We march around Jericho; He levels its walls.

God's guidance comforts in the dying hour. It led the Psalmist to say, "Though I walk through the valley of the shadow of death, I will fear no evil: for thou art with me; thy rod and thy staff they comfort me." The promise Jesus made never to leave or forsake is sweetly fulfilled in death's trying ordeal. When a dear one in great agony was nearing the last moments on earth, I spoke to her of the inscrutable mystery that God should allow His children thus to suffer.

"Oh," said she, "it's all right. We can't see the reason, He can. We are finite, He is infinite," and thus God upheld, and soon she was in the land where suffering cannot come. Hence the Christian triumphantly sings:

And when my task on earth is done,
When, by Thy grace, the victory's won,
E'en death's cold wave I will not flee,
Since God through Jordan leadeth me.

Christ-likeness. All who are divinely led will be like Jesus. Though they have many infirmities which He had not, yet in love, patience, boldness, meekness, and all the graces of a Christian life, they are like Him. The Holy Spirit seeks to bring all to be like Jesus. The Word and providences are the chisels He uses to chip us into the likeness of Jesus. Hence, all who yield to Him are transformed into characters of such beauty as will make angels to marvel.

It is this that enables an eminent saint to testify, "This joyful boldness is grounded on the assurance of a conformity to the image of the Son of God, and that I am through the transfiguring power of the Spirit, like Him in purity, and that the Judge will not condemn facsimiles of Himself, 'because even as He is so are we in this world.' "

Communion with God. They talk with Him and He answers them. Upham, speaking of those who are "truly sanctified," says, "It is not impossible for them to speak, if it is done with a notable degree of reverence, of holding conversation with God, of talking with God. The expression corresponds with the facts. To talk with God, to go to Him familiarly, as children to a parent, to speak to Him in the secrecy of their spirits, and to receive an inward answer, as gracious as it is decisive, is not only a privilege granted them, but a privilege practically realized."

Good works. All who are led by the Spirit will be "always abounding in the work of the Lord." They will be burdened both for the conversion of sinners and the entire sanctification of believers, and will put forth earnest efforts to this end. Coworkers with God, they love His church, and seek to build it up in every rightful way.

Convictions from above, when followed, always lead to success. Other impressions followed may win the favors of friends and temporary satisfaction, but the soul divinely led will have the constant smile of God and of the angels, and "whatsoever he doeth shall prosper." God may lead against armies of opposition and through "Red Seas" of difficulty, "lions' dens" of persecution and "fiery furnaces" of affliction, yet it is always on to sure and final victory.

For such a leader, "Let everything that hath breath praise the Lord."

May we each follow so fully our divine guide that we may be "led safely" in "paths of righteousness" here below, and then be among the blood-bought number of whom it is written, "For the Lamb which is in the midst of the throne shall feed them, and shall lead them unto living fountains of waters: and God shall wipe away all tears from their eyes."

Leaving us an example,
that ye should follow
his steps.

1 PETER 2:21

Man's Perfect Model

Jesus is man's perfect model. The pen portrait of His life which hangs in the gallery of the Gospels should be our constant study. He was a living illustration of the truth which He proclaimed and which we are to practice. He "practiced what He preached," and His glowing example proclaims the practicability of His Gospel.

As there are many men who do not understand the nature of electricity or the laws that govern an electric current, and yet who walk gladly in the beautiful light thus generated, so there are those who are ignorant of the principles and precepts written in the Word, who cannot fail to see their beauty as manifested in the life of Him who is the Light of all worlds, and in whose presence all lesser lights grow dim.

If we will remember the following facts in regard to Him it will aid us greatly in following in His footsteps.

He was just as really and fully human as He was divine. "He took man's nature . . . so that two whole and perfect natures, the Godhead and manhood, were joined together in one person." In the dazzling splendor and majesty of His divine nature men sometimes seem to forget that He was also just as really and intensely human as any other mortal, and that He was the "seed of the woman" as really as the "Son of God." It needs, therefore, to be remembered and emphasized that the King of glory was also the despised Nazarene; that the Creator of all worlds was the helpless babe of Bethlehem's manger; that He who is the Bread of Life was once a hungry, homeless itinerant; that He who is to be the judge of all men was Himself subject to the law; that He who was "declared to be the Son of God with power" was also "a man of sorrows and acquainted with grief"; that He who is to wipe away the tears of others wept and sweat great drops of blood; that He who has the "keys of death" was "obedient unto death"; that He unto whom is given all power in heaven and on earth, was the one who fainted under the weight of the cross as He was led to Calvary, and that "God over all blessed for evermore," was the crucified carpenter.

The humanity of Jesus was just as essential to our salvation as His divinity. Divested of it He would have had no human voice to proclaim His Gospel to us, no tears to shed for us, no blood with which to redeem us, no experience in common with ours to qualify Him to act as our advocate with the Father, and enable Him to sympathize with us in our sorrows and temptations. There would have been no crucifixion and hence no resurrection.

Jesus strongly emphasizes the fact of His humanity by His frequent use, in referring to Himself, of the title, "The Son of man." In Matthew's Gospel alone He uses this title over thirty times, and not once the title, "The Son of God," which was just as truly His. This touching condescension on His part tells of His tender love for us. It is as if a son of the most honorable family in the land, in order to save some poor degraded criminal, would voluntarily lay aside his own honored family name, and cheerfully take that of the outcast thus to prove his affection for him.

110

Blessed Jesus, how immeasurably great is Thy love for fallen man! With glad hearts we embrace Thee, our elder brother, and cherish the blessed thought that the Son of God is also the Son of man. Thus highest heaven stoops to kiss lost earth, and by that kiss conquers it.

Jesus in His humanity, though tempted, was triumphant. He stood on the same fierce battlefield where the first Adam fell, and satanic principalities and powers swept down upon Him in mighty squadrons, until "tempted in all points like as we are," He was tested, but put to flight His every foe, and before the onlooking universe was victor. His humanity resting with an unfaltering faith upon the rock of the divine was mighty to resist every satanic shock. Thus anchored He was safe, and so long as we, like Him, "do these things we shall never fall."

It is our privilege and our duty to be like Jesus. There are so many ways in which we cannot be like Him that this may blind our eyes to the ways in which we can. We cannot be like Him, nor does He expect it in many of the incidental circumstances of His life, nor in the possession of His divine attributes. Nor can we with our dwarfed physical, mental, and spiritual powers be like Him in the keenness of His perceptions and in His ability and promptness in applying the truth to personal experience. His mind could detect an error and leap to a right conclusion in an instant, where ours, hampered by a defective memory, imperfect knowledge, and by many other infirmities from which He was free, must pass through a long, and perhaps laborious process. Yet in the following particulars we can and should be like Him:

1. He was the blameless Son of God; we should be "sons of God without rebuke."

2. He was obedient; we should keep His commandments.

3. He was self-denying; we should deny ourselves, take up our cross, and follow Him.

4. He pleased the Father; we should "walk worthy of the Lord unto all pleasing."

5. He was tempted on all points like as we are, yet without sin; we, too, must be tempted, and if we resist the devil he will flee from us.

6. He forgave His enemies; we are to forgive if we would be forgiven.

7. He loved us while we were in rebellion against Him; we are to love our enemies, and like Him, to pray for them.

8. He was pure in heart; "He that hath this hope in him purifieth himself even as he is pure."

9. He was the Light of the world; if we follow Him we "shall not walk in darkness, but shall have the light of life."

10. He always knew the Father's will; "all His sheep" may "know His voice."

11. He was baptized with the Holy Ghost; we are to tarry until we receive "the promise of the Father."

12. He was persecuted—the servant is not above His Lord; to be a genuine Christian is to be persecuted.

13. He engaged in no filthy or injurious habit; we are to "cleanse ourselves from all filthiness of the flesh and spirit."

14. He never allied Himself to worldlings; we are to come out from among them and be separate.

15. He always put the Father's interest first; we, too, are to "seek first the kingdom."

16. Jesus was "bold, energetic, decided, courageous"; no one denies that all His followers should be.

17. In regard to personal matters He was flexible, submissive, and yielding; His followers in this respect are exhorted to be kind, tenderhearted, and in honor to prefer one another.

18. Though He was rich, yet for our sakes He became poor; He declared of His followers that "whosoever he be of you that forsaketh not all that he hath, he cannot be my disciple." Our forsaking all is like emptying our hands of dross that God may fill them with diamonds.

19. He abounded in good and mighty works; it is written, "He that believeth on me, the works that I do shall he do also; and greater works than these shall he do; because I go unto my Father."

20. He died; so must all His followers.

21. He rose again; "as we have borne the image of the earthy, we shall also bear the image of the heavenly."

22. He shall reign forever; He "hast made us unto our God kings and priests: and we shall reign on the earth."

In all the above, and many more particulars, it is clearly declared that all His followers are like Him. May the Holy Spirit fix in all our hearts the blessed truth that "His example is strictly and exactly an example for all the world." When tempted to diverge from the path of duty, or to condone sin "because we are human," let us remember that Jesus, too, was human, and that while His Gospel does not save us from our humanity, nor while in this world from our infirmities, yet, if fully received, it will save us from our sins. Our transformation into the likeness of Jesus is the great object of His Gospel. For this He shed His precious blood, and gives His renewing and sanctifying Spirit. Without these, man could no more be like Jesus than a leopard could be like a lamb. The unregenerate man who tries to be like Jesus by doing religious acts and good works is simply a human leopard under a lamb's skin. First, we must be transformed into His image, and then having thus been made like Him we will be enabled to "walk as he walked," and in our little sphere as the drop bears the image of the ocean, and the

113

ray of light the image of the sun, so shall we reflect
His likeness. This is our privilege here and now. By and
by, "soul and body shall His glorious image bear."

Next, let us bear in mind that Jesus in His humanity is
the Christian's model, in regard to being divinely led.
His every act and word bear each of the stamps that prove
them from the skies.

Jesus never said or did an unscriptural thing. Though
born of the Spirit, filled with the Spirit, and led by the
Spirit, Jesus continually recognized the Scriptures as the
rule of His conduct, and always magnified the written
Word.

His mistaken followers who claim that the Spirit may
lead contrary to the Bible should learn this much-needed
lesson from the Great Teacher.

The very fact that the Holy Spirit is the author of
Scripture proves that all His teachings and leadings will be
in accord with it; for an infinitely wise author will not
contradict Himself. Jesus revered the written Word as a
dutiful son reveres the will of a dear father; and when He
made new revelations they were simply the unfolding of
the old, and were to them what the blossom and fruitage
is to the bud.

His miraculous advent, the angel's message to Mary, to
Joseph, and to the shepherd, and all of the great events
of His life, were foretold in Scripture and in harmony with
it. His chief employment when a youth doubtless was the
mastery of Bible truth; and in later years it was with
the "Sword of the Spirit" that He pierced the formality and
hypocrisy of a haughty ecclesiasticism. When tempted
in the wilderness to distrust God and use unlawful means
to satisfy His hunger, like men do when they do wrong
for a livelihood; and when tempted to test God's power by
doing a presumptuous thing; and when tempted to give
up His divine mission for gain, like men do when they

turn from the ministry or from principle, for money or position; and, finally, when tempted to own the lordship of the devil by worshiping him; in each instance He tried the satanic suggestion by the written Word, and thrusting the enemy through with the keen blade of a fitting Scripture quotation He put him to flight, and "angels came and ministered unto him."

The miracles He wrought, the prophecies He fulfilled, the glad tidings He proclaimed, the denunciations He uttered, His betrayal, trial, crucifixion, resurrection, ascension, and reign, all were foretold and in harmony with the Scriptures. When human opposers accused Him of violating the Word, He always successfully defended Himself and exposed their deception and error. He was never like them and some of His professed followers today, guilty of wresting Scripture from its proper place and meaning to serve a selfish purpose. In His boyhood, though His young heart burned to be about His Father's business, yet He restrained His "strong impressions," and, as taught in the law of Moses, was subject unto His parents. Thus by His example He taught that impulses which, if followed, would lead to disobedience, should be smothered.

When He engaged in the extraordinary act of scourging the buyers and sellers from the temple, and commanded them no more to make His Father's house a place of merchandise, He met their indignant opposition by the unanswerable Bible declaration: "It is written, my house shall be called the house of prayer; but ye have made it a den of thieves."

Thus at every step He rested the rightfulness of His acts upon the written Word. Study the Gospels with reference to the allusions of Jesus to Scripture, and you doubtless will be surprised at their frequency.

In the presence of the luminous example of our divine model, the fatal fallacy proclaimed by some that the Holy

Ghost may lead to do deeds which are unscriptural and contrary to sanctified common sense, dies a death that knows no resurrection. To follow it is to stumble into its grave.

As His life work was the working out of God's will concerning Him as it is revealed in the Word, so in our humble spheres shall ours be. May we ever fully follow in His steps.

He never said or did a wrong thing. All His words and acts were right. Tried by the most rigid criticism of friend and foe, no wrong act has ever been proved against Him. The candid verdict of the centuries is voiced in Pilate's words: "I find no fault in this man." His most malignant foes, who watched Him with eagle eyes for years, at last gave up the fruitless search, and hired false witnesses to manufacture charges against Him of crimes which it was impossible for them to find. All agree that it is right to do good continually and to all, and this was His life work: "He went about doing good." All agree that it is right to expose fraud and rebuke hypocrisy. This He did repeatedly, thoroughly, and fearlessly. Every act of His wonderful life was so manifestly right that He, without fear of the results, could triumphantly challenge His enemies: "Which of you convinceth me of sin?" Through His wondrous power may we each claim the grace that will lead us, like Him, to be so busy in doing good that we will have no time nor inclination for that which is wrong or even questionable.

He never said or did an unreasonable thing. He was always reasonable. He was so manifestly so that His bitterest foes seldom disputed His logic, and when they did, they fell confounded beneath its lightnings. His replies so exposed their ignorance and revealed His own wisdom, that, dumfounded, they "could not answer him again to those things," "and after that they durst not ask him

116

any questions at all." His doctrines, His requirements of His followers, and His own life were all in harmony with the cool conclusions of a spiritually enlightened judgment. Notice the illustration of this in a few of the incidents of His life:

1. His temptation in the wilderness. If He was to succor and sympathize with weak, tempted humanity, was it not reasonable that He, weak, exhausted, and alone, should meet and vanguish severe temptations? If the written Word is the weapon which must be wielded to defeat the enemy, is it not reasonable that our Great Exampler should embrace an occasion to teach us how to use it?

2. His plan of propagating the Gospel. Could any more reasonable time for opening His ministry be suggested than that which He chose, in the very height of John's popularity, when the multitudes were thronging him, and the nation was awakened, and religious thought was at high tide as the result of the startling utterances of the new Elijah? Have any more reasonable methods for proclaiming the truth, and getting and holding the attention of a nation ever been found than His plain, pointed preaching, combined with the miraculous deeds of mercy which He gratuitously performed, and His fearless arraignment of the formalists of His day? Can we conceive of a more admirable plan for the work He had to do than His, or sending out "simultaneously a number of His most cordial friends and followers to assist in making the most powerful impression possible on the community"? Does not the sequel prove that He chose the most reasonable time, methods, and men for the accomplishments of His work?

Do not His public trial, crucifixion, resurrection, ascension, and the gifts with which He has endowed his followers present the most effective and rational plan for the purpose designed that possibly can be conceived of?

The rationality of Jesus' methods were unwittingly eulogized by the famous French wit, to whom a religious enthusiast came for advice about introducing a new religion. "Be crucified and rise again the third day," was the sarcastic, yet forceful counsel.

Was it not reasonable also that Jesus should further enforce the truth of His Gospel by practicing what He preached? Did He not do this? What a contrast in this particular between Him and the hypocritical pretenders of that age and this! He not only proclaimed the importance of prayer, fasting, self-denial, and personal work, but faultlessly exemplified these and all other truths which he preached. In these and all other particulars of His wonderful life He was always in harmony with an enlightened reason. Calm, self-possessed, and luminous with holy light, He shines forth the great central sun in the Gospel system, marred by no spots of ridiculous speech or action. May His misguided followers who are prompted to do absurd things in His name study more clearly this phase of His character, and then aim to be like Him.

Jesus' life was always in harmony with providential events. Providential opportunities to perform the deeds that the Spirit prompted Him to do sprang up as by magic before His coming steps. He came in contact with the occasions and persons essential to His success as naturally as a magnet draws the steel. He never was guilty of the inconsistency of feeling that it was God's will that He should do things which God's providences did not allow Him to do. Forbidding circumstances which appall timid souls that know not the secret of God's full grace and guidance, to Him, as to all who will follow in His steps, proved golden chariots to bear Him up the heights of victory. Infuriated fellow townsmen, ecclesiastical intrigue, and Roman power combined were unable to stop Him in the discharge of a single duty; but each in its way was made to contribute

to His glory. He walked so fully in the providential path
marked out for Him that there was not a single jar between
Him and the events He daily met. Thus His life proves a
forceful reminder that the door of providential opportunity
always swings open before him whom God leads. May we
continue to look to the "Model Man" until, like Him,
our lives are thus adjusted to God's providential dealings.

*Jesus always fully met the conditions of being divinely
led*. His humanity reposed in the lap of the divine. Dead
to the world, saved from self, filled with the Spirit, always
putting the interests of the kingdom first, and unhesitatingly
following every prompting from above, no matter how
great the cost to Himself, the life of Jesus hangs in the
gallery of the centuries as "Man's Perfect Model" of meeting
the conditions of heavenly guidance.

*All the rich results of being divinely led find full fruition
in the life of Jesus*. Possessed of all of the fruits of the
Spirit, His life was a perfect representation of true manhood
as God designed it to be.

Although such a cloudburst of trial, opposition,
accusation, and suffering fell upon Him as no other man
ever knew, yet, amid it all, he was never envious, irritable,
haughty, self-willed, hurried, disappointed, or perplexed.

Let us examine a few of the "fruits of Canaan" which
grew in the garden of the life of our "Perfect Model,"
and remember that kindred fruits will abound in all who
are fully possessed of His Spirit. As the pupil learns of the
perfect example which he seeks to copy, so being made
like Jesus, may we look to and learn of Him.

He was humble. This was strikingly manifest in His
subjection to His parents and to ordinances, to the indignities
that were heaped upon Him, to poverty, and in His
acceptance of His humble lot, and in other ways which
have been mentioned. To all who follow Him He says,
"Take my yoke upon you and learn of me; for I am meek

and lowly in heart, and ye shall find rest to your souls."

He was obedient. He did the Father's will even as He taught us to pray, "as it is done in heaven." He did it promptly, cheerfully, continually. Whether it was to speak words of healing and of comfort or to suffer on the cross, He was obedient, and obedient unto death. Seeing from the beginning all the shame, reproach, hatred, and agony that was in the pathway of obedience which lay before Him, yet He could say, "I delight to do thy will, O my God."

He was tried. In the wilderness by the devil, at home by His kindred and fellow townsmen, in His public life by the ridicule, deception, intrigue, and opposition of His enemies, and the cowardice, selfish ambition, and misdirected zeal of His friends, on every side and in all points He was tempted as we are, yet without sin. It is said that a man once came to Napoleon claiming to have made bulletproof armor. "Put it on," said the general. He did so. Turning to an orderly, Napoleon ordered him to fire. The inventor refused to allow his boasted armor thus to be tested. Jesus has made a coat of mail which He declares will turn aside "all the fiery darts of the wicked." He wore it while here below, and proved its perfection.

He was calm, self-possessed, and assured. He illustrated the inspired declaration that "the work of righteousness shall be peace, and the effect of righteousness quietness and assurance forever." Whether He was in the temple teaching and asking questions, on the mountainside preaching to the multitudes, in humble homes working miracles, before Pilate falsely accused, or suffering on the cruel cross, the whole tenor of His life was like the quiet flow of some deep and mighty stream. The overflow of feeling, such as He manifested in regard to the desecration of the temple, the hypocrisy of the priesthood, and at

Gethsemane, were the exceptions and not the rule of His life.

He was a man of sorrow. People who in their zeal to condemn a long-faced religion, eliminate from their creed and lives the sorrow such as Jesus felt for fallen man, and such as comes from the cross-bearing and self-denial which He imposes, need to study more closely their divine model.

> *All things seemed*
> *To fight against Him, heaven was black with clouds,*
> *And terrible upon the mountains shone*
> *The feet of hurrying storms; the rapid glance*
> *Of scattered lightnings; then the thunders loud*
> *Broke on that lonely sea, and on the men*
> *Who walked thereon; then met upon His head*
> *The sorrows of eternal death, and none*
> *For whom He died were found to comfort Christ.*

It is only those who suffer with Him who shall reign with Him.

Jesus was possessed of a deep, abiding joy. Though sorrowful, He was always rejoicing. This joy He bequeaths to all His followers. He says,"That my joy might remain in you, and that your joy might be full."

As near as we can learn, the joy of Jesus consisted, as Adam Clark says, in "fulfilling the will of the Father in tasting death for every man." This, with the anticipation of the rapture it would bring to countless multitudes, was His joy, or at least a fruitful source of it, and a kindred self-sacrifice and anticipation of its results in blessing to others will possess all in whom the Spirit dwells. Its manifestation in the life of Jesus was hid beneath the agonizing efforts of pain and loss with which His life was filled in rescuing the race; but the consciousness of His Father's continual approbation and the success of His soul-saving work were wellsprings of joy even in His hours of deepest agony. "For the joy that was set before Him [He] endured the cross, despising the shame, and is set down at the right hand of the throne of God" (Hebrews 12:2).

Great success was preceded by great agony. His early ministry was preceded by His humble birth, misunderstood parentage, and the terrible temptation in the wilderness. His public efforts were opposed at every step by persistent and wily foes. Many of the ministry and church members of His day looked upon Him with suspicion and hatred. Even His "own brethren did not believe on Him." The resurrection and Pentecost were preceded by Gethsemane and the crucifixion. He endured untold agony upon the bloody battlefield before He could wear the victor's crown. Beloved, "let this mind be in you, which was also in Christ Jesus: who, being in the form of God, thought it not robbery to be equal with God: but made himself of no reputation, and took upon him the form of a servant, and was made in the likeness of men: and being found in fashion as a man, he humbled himself, and became obedient unto death, even the death of the cross. Wherefore God also hath highly exalted him, and given him a name which is above every name: that at the name of Jesus every knee should bow, . . . and that every tongue should confess that Jesus Christ is Lord, to the glory of God the Father" (Philippians 2:5-11).

It is a part of God's plan that every resurrection and Pentecost shall be preceded by a Gethsemane and Calvary. The Holy Spirit fully followed will sustain in the conflict, and lead to the crown. Instead of being surprised at opposition in the path of duty, it should be remembered that our "Perfect Model" met it, and that, like Him, we are to expect, meet, and conquer it.

Jesus was patient. His patience must have been sorely tried by the stupidity, rashness, and carnality of His followers, by the treachery of Judas, by the inconveniences that were inseparable from His homeless life, by the weariness and weakness that came from exposure, hunger, fasting, and toilsome journeys from place to place; yet not one impatient word ever fell from His lips.

Jesus proclaimed the plain truth. He insisted on the necessity of repentance and of the new birth; emphasized man's accountability, the judgment and the reality of heaven, and the awfulness and duration of the doom of the damned.

He preached against the popular sins of his day. Neither the priesthood nor common people who were living in public or private sin escaped His denunciations. His lightning leaped upon hypocritical ecclesiastics with gleeful fury. Like their brethren today, who love the praise of men more than the praise of God, and seek more earnestly the honors of earth than the gift of the Holy Ghost, they doubtless dubbed Him a "scolding pessimist," and followed their own ways instead of His truth.

Jesus was possessed of deep, filial affection. This was manifested in the provision He made for His precious mother at the crucifixion. All who like Him are led and indwelt by the Spirit will, like Him, love their kindred. His Gospel turns the hearts of parents to their children and the hearts of children to their parents. I know of a woman who was once a loving, dutiful daughter. She gave up the Gospel for the "mind cure" craze, and it froze up her affections for her saintly mother so that she treats her cruelly. A system which does this has not Jesus for its author. Union with Him expels every false affection, but intensifies every lawful love.

Jesus lived a life of prayer. He taught that prayer was the key with which man unlocks the bank of divine

blessings. By His example He shows us how to use it.
Praying earnestly, persistently, and with pure motives, He
always prevailed. Alone in the Garden of Gethsemane,
and sometimes all night long on the damp mountainside,
Jesus communed and interceded with the Father. One
proof of His humanity is that He needed thus to pray. If
He had been only divine, with no humanity, it would
not have been so. If Jesus thus prayed in order to fulfill
His mission, much more must we. All whose lives are
molded by convictions from above will, like Him, be
possessed of a spirit which "prays without ceasing," and
will be led to be much alone with God in prayer.

Jesus was fearless. Bravest of earth's heroes, He faced
danger in every form, and never fled for fear. Before
His "time was come" He sometimes wisely evaded an issue
which would have been profitless, as when His fellow
townsmen sought His life at the close of His first public
address at Nazareth; but on such occasions it was for
prudential reasons, and not for lack of courage that He
fled. He met the treachery and infidelity of professed
friends and the secret conspiracies of His open foes with
the same spirit of fortitude. The heroism He manifested in
the calm courage with which He met Judas and his
murderous band is not surpassed in the annals of history.
He was not excited, but calm and self-possessed. He knew
that His life was sought. He knew that it would be taken.
He had power to defeat the murderous conspiracy and
destroy all who were engaged in it, yet He forbore to use
it, and in the livid glare of the torchlights which seemed
to dance with fiendish glee over the triumph of wrong,
He faced His foes with a majesty that struck them to the
earth. He marched as self-possessed to His trial as a king
to his throne. It was toward His throne in the affections
of ransomed millions. The perfect love, which casts out
fear, and which is a part of His legacy to all who serve

Him, was enthroned within, and made Him brave to face all perils, only that He might accomplish His mission from the skies and redeem a loved but apostate race. When that love in its purity and perfection sways His followers, they, like Him, are brave to face all storms, and are entered on the list of the heroes of the universe, of whom He is the honored leader.

He was glorified. A little while in the crucible of trial, and then an eternity of infinite glory! A brief, stormy voyage on the rough sea of human life, and then forever in the heavenly haven with the countless multitudes whom He has rescued! To Him death was simply "glorification," and through Him it likewise is to all who follow fully in His steps. If true to Him we "shall never see death," but, like Him, when our work here is done, we shall be glorified. Hallelujah!

In Him then we see the perfect manhood which results from His indwelling in human hearts, and the blessed life of trial and victory which comes to those who are controlled by "convictions from above."

In Jesus, "Man's Perfect Model," we see with clear vision the steps our humanity must take to meet the end for which it was created:

Humanity obedient—Jesus doing the Father's will.

Humanity tempted—Jesus and the temptation.

Humanity humbled—Jesus suffering for the salvation of others.

Humanity triumphant—Jesus and the resurrection.

Humanity exalted—Jesus ascending to the right hand of the Father.

These are the steps in which we are to follow our illustrious leader to our prepared place above.

The writer is aware that he has but imperfectly pointed to "Man's Perfect Model," and only to a few of the many brilliant stars that shine in the constellation of His matchless graces. He trusts that all imperfections of expression may be lost sight of in the light of Him whose grace and beauty he has sought to magnify. His earnest prayer for all who read these pages is: "That ye might be filled with the knowledge of his will in all wisdom and spiritual understanding; that ye might walk worthy of the Lord unto all pleasing, being fruitful in every good work, and increasing in the knowledge of God; strengthened with all might, according to his glorious power, unto all patience and longsuffering with joyfulness; giving thanks unto the Father, which hath made us meet to be partakers of the inheritance of the saints in light: who hath delivered us from the power of darkness, and hath translated us into the kingdom of his dear Son," to whom be honor, and power, and glory forever.

Praise God, from whom all blessings flow;
Praise Him all creatures here below;
Praise Him above, ye heavenly host;
Praise Father, Son, and Holy Ghost.